H·O·T
(Hands-On Transactional)
MANAGEMENT

Bruce Tulgan

HRD PRESS
Amherst, Massachusetts

Copyright © 2004, Bruce Tulgan

Published by: HRD Press, Inc.
                22 Amherst Road
                Amherst, MA 01002
                800-822-2801 (U.S. and Canada)
                413-253-3488
                413-253-3490 (fax)
                http://www.hrdpress.com

ISBN: 0-87425-795-6

Cover design by Eileen Klockars
Editorial and production services by Mary George

Dedication

*To Jeff Coombs, my business partner
at RainmakerThinking, the best
HOT manager I've ever known, and one of
my very best friends in the world*

Contents

Acknowledgments

AS ALWAYS, I must thank first and foremost the many thousands of managers and individual contributors who, since 1993, have shared with RainmakerThinking the lessons of their workplace experiences. Every interview has been a learning opportunity and many have been profound. I am grateful to every single one of you for taking the time to share your voice. HOT Management would not have been possible without you.

I am also indebted to all the business leaders and managers who have expressed so much confidence in our work and given us the opportunity to learn from the real management issues they deal with and solve on a daily basis. Thank you for all that you have taught me and for the chance to work with such fine people. I am honored to be included in your efforts to make your organizations even better than they are.

To the tens of thousands who have attended my seminars: As I have said before, thanks for listening, for laughing, for kindly sharing the wisdom of your experience, for pushing me with the really tough questions, and for continually teaching me.

As our partnership with HRD Press grows, I am ever more grateful to publisher Bob Carkhuff and his team for our close working relationship and their ongoing confidence in me and our work at RainmakerThinking. Special thanks also to Mary George, who does such great editing and design work on our books published by HRD Press.

To my colleagues at RainmakerThinking, especially the other principals here, Carolyn Martin and Jeff Coombs: Thank you for your hard work and commitment, and for the valuable contributions you make to this enterprise every single day. Carolyn teaches me so much every time I come within earshot of her: She is a brilliant thinker, speaker, and trainer, and a wonderful human being. This book is dedicated to Jeff because he is my poster child for HOT Management. Jeff is a great guy—a good listener who's smart, kind, wise, and highly articulate—but he hated the idea of being a supervisor and having to tell employees what to do and then hold them accountable. So step by step, he learned and practiced the techniques of HOT Management. Every single day, he spent time coaching every single one of our employees, one person at a time—and still does. Now Jeff is as skilled a manager as I've ever known—and living proof that HOT Management can be learned and mastered even by those who must be dragged kicking and screaming into the enterprise.

Finally, I owe extraordinary thanks, for innumerable reasons, to my entire family and so many of my wonderful friends. And, as always, I reserve my deepest thanks for my wife, Dr. Debby Applegate, who is the love of my life and my partner in all things.

Introduction

EVERYWHERE I GO, people in supervisory positions tell me the same thing: "It's getting harder and harder to manage people." Why is that so?

Managers in every workplace today are caught in a tug of war. On one side are the employers, demanding more work and better work out of people—often fewer people than they once had, with fewer resources as well. On the other side are the employees, feeling pressured and overworked, wanting some relief in the form of flexible working conditions, or at least some incentive to continue their hard work. Stuck in the middle—trying to negotiate these competing needs—is every single person with supervisory authority.

How can managers reconcile these opposite forces? How can they possibly win the game? What can they do every day to get more work and better work out of each person and at the same time give people more of the flexibility they need?

HOT Management provides an answer to those questions. I coined the term "HOT Management" to describe the highly engaged management style, techniques, skills, best practices, and habits of the most effective supervisory managers in today's extremely demanding workplace. "HOT" is an acronym for "hands-on transactional"—the key to this successful approach.

The fundamental principle of HOT Management is that work is a transaction between employees and managers—one that requires supervisory hands-on strategies in place of outmoded hierarchical tactics. "Transactional" means there is a quid pro quo for everything:

- If employees want rewards, they must perform.

- The more employees perform, the more rewards they receive.

- Good performance is the only option.

Equally important is the emphasis on supervising with a "hands-on," rather than "hands-off," approach. There are three crucial requirements for managers:

- They must be extremely knowledgeable about the work their direct reports are doing.

- They must spend a lot of time with direct reports, spelling out expectations, clarifying standards, and defining goals and deadlines.

- They must have the guts to hold their direct reports accountable.

Our research indicates that when managers take this hands-on transactional approach, they can do much more *for* employees while also requiring much more *from* employees. As a result, everyone benefits. Productivity, quality, and morale levels soar, as well as the retention rates of top-notch performers.

HOT Management is a straightforward method designed to teach anyone with supervisory responsibility the key techniques of the most effective supervisors in today's workplace. With practice, these techniques will become a habit, leading to the development of HOT Management skills. And the results will follow.

Where Does HOT Management Come From?

HOT Management is based on ongoing workplace research at my firm, RainmakerThinking, Inc. In 1993, I initiated a series of in-depth employee interviews focused on the changing values, norms, and practices in the workplace. More than a decade later, with help from my colleagues, I am still conducting that research. In the course of our work, we have interviewed more than ten thousand individuals, studied the management practices of 700 organizations, held dozens of focus groups, polled thousands of respondents, reviewed internal survey data from 300 organizations (reflecting more than a million respondents), and led over a thousand interactive seminars with hundreds of thousands of participants.

We've tracked the incredible shifts in the workplace from the early days of downsizing, restructuring, and reengineering through the tech boom, the dot-com craze, and the economic downturn of the early 2000s. And we've seen changes that go way beyond short-term trends and ordinary fluctuations in the labor market. There is a historic macro-economic shift under way. Driven by the great forces of technology and globalization, the larger economy has reached a new stage of global interconnection, high speed, and complexity. The worldwide business environment has become one of high risk, erratic markets, and unpredictable resource needs. In order to adjust, organizations of all sizes have tried to become more lean and flexible. Without credible long-term promises from employers, most employees work anxiously to take care of themselves and their families and try to get what they can from their employers—one day at a time.

The traditional long-term hierarchical employer-employee bond has morphed into a short-term transactional relationship. Employees these days constantly seem to ask: "What's the deal around here? What do you want from me? And what do I get for my hard work—today?" While many managers still find this attitude frustrating and downright maddening, our research indicates that today's most effective managers are actually embracing it. They realize that employees are more likely to cooperate and to perform at higher levels when supervisors tie rewards and detriments directly to clear goals and deadlines. This only works, though, when managers are generous and even-handed while also being extremely rigorous: setting clear expectations, correcting performance problems immediately, and quickly removing low-level performers from the workplace. It is this set of techniques, skills, and habits that we call HOT Management.

Why Does HOT Management Work So Well in Today's Workplace?

In the current workplace, new sources of authority are quickly supplanting the traditional ones. Seniority, age, rank, and rules are diminishing in value. Organization charts are flatter, as layers of management have been removed. Reporting relationships are more temporary, with an ever greater number of employees managed by short-term project-leaders instead of "organization-chart" managers. These changes have led to the rise of more transactional sources of authority, such as control of resources, control of rewards, and control of work conditions.

Managers are thus losing their old-fashioned, long-term hierarchical power. But they are also gaining many opportunities to draw on new sources of short-term transactional power.

Increasingly, managers are not only the primary points of contact for most employees, but also, on a daily basis, the ones who define the work experience. Employees rely on immediate supervisors more than anyone else for meeting their basic needs and expectations and handling a whole range of day-to-day issues. These include the assignment of tasks, resource planning, problem solving, training, scheduling, dispute resolution, guidance, coaching, recognition, and promotions and other rewards. It is the immediate supervisor to whom an employee turns, whether seeking a special assignment, needing vital resources, pursuing an optimum work location, avoiding a certain coworker, looking for a good performance evaluation, or hoping for a raise.

The managers we call HOT are letting go of the old power and embracing the new. Their strategies include:

- Driving performance through negotiation and coaching

- Focusing on their immediate sphere of authority and influence (and generally ignoring what they have little control over, such as bureaucracy and red tape)

- Gaining power by positioning themselves as the ones who can do more for people

- Doing what it takes to gain control of discretionary resources—and then using those resources as bargaining chips with employees

- Relying on interpersonal communication skills as a source of power

- Engaging direct reports in ongoing coaching dialogues about performance standards, goals, and deadlines

- Remembering that flexibility and accountability go hand in hand

- Having the guts to hold every person accountable every day.

That's how HOT managers increase productivity and quality one person at a time, one day at a time.

What's in This Pocket Guide?

Over the last few years, I've shared the HOT Management approach with thousands of leaders and managers in hundreds of organizations, from the CIA to TGI Friday's. The response has been so positive that we've created a HOT Management training program, available on CD-ROM from RainmakerThinking or HRD Press. (For further details, visit www.rainmakerthinking.com or log on to www.hrdpress.com.) Now we're offering this pocket guide as the latest in our line of HRD Press books and programs.

The pocket guide includes all of the following:

- Clear and simple explanations of the HOT Management approach

- Examples from real-life work situations

- Room for brainstorming along the way

- Concrete techniques for daily coaching, performance improvement, removing low performers, and rewarding high performers

HOT Management is about the day-to-day relationships you have with the individuals you manage. Are you ready to . . .

— take responsibility for being a better manager?

— spend more time with every person you manage?

— hold clearly focused conversations every day with every person about performance standards and concrete goals and deadlines?

— hold every person accountable, one day at a time?

— deal with performance problems immediately from now on?

— remove recalcitrant low-level performers from your team?

— cut through the bureaucracy and red tape?

— create an intense, high-performing team and then maintain the intensity?

Read this book. Try out the techniques. Turn those techniques into skills and habits. It won't take you long to see that HOT Management may be high maintenance, but it works.

1

What Is HOT Management?

SUPPORTED BY OVER a decade of research, HOT Management is a straightforward approach to high-performance supervision based on the techniques and habits of the most effective supervisory managers in today's high-pressure, high-maintenance workplace. HOT Management captures the philosophy and techniques of supervisory managers with soaring productivity, great morale, and low turnover among high performers. In theory, it's very simple; but in practice, it can be challenging, often requiring a huge adjustment for managers. The results make that challenge worth meeting.

To understand HOT Management, it's important to be clear on what we mean by "hands-on" and "transactional," which together give us the acronym HOT. In this chapter, we will take a close look at these two components. First, though, I would like to clarify what we mean by "management."

Many people have wondered why the term "manage-ment" is used for this approach. Are we making a choice, seeing management as distinct from leadership and supervision? Not at all.

I know that there are volumes of research that make such distinctions: leaders focus on the big picture, managers on details, supervisors on carrying out the details; leaders inspire, managers do paperwork, and supervisors assign, monitor, and measure the tasks of individual contributors. But the truth of the matter is, there are *no* major dividing lines between leadership and management and supervision.

If you are in a position of authority and influence and you have employees reporting to you, then you should be focusing on the big picture, inspiring others, focus-ing on details, doing the paperwork, and making sure all the work gets done. I don't care if you call yourself a leader, a manager, or a supervisor: I'm talking about you. And HOT Management is designed for you.

Being "Hands-On" and "Transactional"

Exactly what does it mean to be "hands-on"? Likewise, what does it mean to be "transactional"? The balance of this chapter answers those questions. However, it is essential to keep in mind that these two components are integrally related: *Success depends on both.* If you're going to be hands-on in today's workplace, you had better be transactional, offering concrete incentives every step of the way. And if you're going to be transactional, you had better be hands-on, spelling out expectations at every step, monitoring and measuring performance, and holding people accountable. Keep this in mind as we examine each component.

What Does It Mean to Be "Hands-On"?

Being hands-on means all of the following:

1. Being highly knowledgeable about the tasks and responsibilities of your direct reports

2. Spending time with every direct report in daily coaching sessions

3. Using your coaching time with direct reports to talk about the work they are doing

4. Providing direction, guidance, and support on a regular basis

5. Monitoring and measuring performance in writing, so that you can reward success and address failure

Let's take a closer look at each of these definitions.

1. Being Highly Knowledgeable About the Tasks and Responsibilities of Your Direct Reports

To be "highly knowledgeable," you must know the details of your people's work. Does this mean you have to know every detail? No, not every detail, of course. Then how much detail?

- Enough to know . . .
  - — what can be done every day, and what cannot
  - — what resources will be necessary
  - — what problems may occur
  - — what expectations are reasonable
  - — what goals and deadlines are sufficiently ambitious
- Enough to fairly and accurately monitor and measure success and failure

At the very least, you should know what your direct reports expect you to know. Ideally, you should be so grounded in the details that your direct reports are not even sure where your knowledge ends. You want them to think, "Gee, my boss seems to know everything about what I'm doing. How does this person keep track of it all?"

2. Spending Time With Every Direct Report in Daily Coaching Sessions

Does this mean every single day? Ideally, but there is room for flexibility. Every direct report is different. Some require more time more often. Others require less time less often. Not only that, but work is a moving target: Some tasks and responsibilities and projects require more time more often; others require less time less often. If you are sufficiently hands-on, you should be able to gauge how much time you need to spend with each direct report, depending upon the person and his or her tasks, responsibilities, and projects.

We have two rules of thumb:

- In an ideal world, you would have a brief, 15-minute coaching session with every direct report every single day.

- *At the very least,* you should have a brief coaching session with every direct report once a week.

3. Using Your Coaching Time With Direct Reports to Talk About the Work They Are Doing

Isn't it important to talk about things other than work? It may be. But if you have limited time, your first priority should be talking about the work. If you don't have time for a 15-minute coaching session with every direct report every day, then in the limited time you *do* spend with each direct report, stay focused on the work.

Talking about the work means reminding direct reports about overall performance standards and, more important, spelling out concrete expectations. You must clarify daily (or weekly) goals and deadlines. You must articulate guidelines and parameters. Your mantra in your daily (or weekly) meetings should be "Here's what I need you to do: [*specific goal*]. I need this by [*specific deadline*]. And here are the guidelines: [*specific directions*]. Do you understand?"

4. Providing Direction, Guidance, and Support on a Regular Basis

In your regular meetings, you must be prepared to help identify resource needs and help fulfill them. You must be prepared to help identify potential problems and help solve them. You must be prepared to monitor and measure the workload of each person so that you can put the pressure on or take the pressure off as needed. You must be prepared to evaluate performance so that you can determine when tasks, responsibilities, and projects are a good fit or a bad fit; when a direct report requires more information or additional training; when a direct report is having a bad day, or a good day; when a direct report needs advice, motivation, inspiration, or counsel.

5. Monitoring and Measuring Performance in Writing, So That You Can Reward Success and Address Failure

You must be in a position to judge the cause of success as well as failure, and be able to determine whether that cause is linked to a direct report's attention, care, judgment, or effort. You must also be able to document your judgment. That means you must routinely keep notes during every coaching session with every direct report. Record the performance standards and expectations that are communicated, the goals and deadlines that are assigned, and all other significant details as they are discussed.

✦ The Question of Micro-Management Versus Empowerment

Is hands-on management the same as micro-management? No, it is just plain management. There has been so much emphasis on empowerment in recent years, and fear of micro-management, that managers have moved too far afield of providing direction. If you want to empower direct reports, you must define the terrain in which they have power.

THE CIRCLE OF EMPOWERMENT

That terrain consists of effectively delegated goals with clear guidelines and concrete deadlines, as illustrated by the Circle of Empowerment, above. The smaller the circle, the more often you have to meet with your direct report. The larger the circle, the less often you have to meet (but at least once a week).

It is within the circle's terrain that a direct report has power. For example, let's say you delegate the following: "I want you to create a box by Tuesday at 3 p.m. It must be smaller than a refrigerator and bigger than a breadbox. It can't be yellow, but it could be gold—do you know the difference between yellow and gold? Do you understand my directions?" Here you have a goal, a deadline, and guidelines. Within those parameters, a direct report has all the power. For instance, the box could be any shape (round, oblong, octagonal, etc.) and almost any color.

For more on delegation and empowerment, see the next page.

> ## ✦ Delegation and the Circle of Empowerment
>
> Mastering the articulation of goals, deadlines, and guidelines is mastering the art of effective delegation. That is the hard work of managing people. If you don't do that work, you are not empowering people, but neglecting them. And if you do that work, you are not micro-managing.
>
> With each person and instance of delegation, the trick is to figure out three basic things: How large should the goal be? How far out should the deadline be? And how many guidelines are necessary? In other words, how big should the terrain ("circle") of empowerment be?
>
> Here is the answer: As a direct report demonstrates proficiency, enlarge the circle a bit at a time until you reach the person's appropriate sphere of responsibility. If a new project comes up or you must increase productivity and quality, it is usually best to shrink the circle. And if a performance problem develops, shrink the circle until the problem is corrected.

What Does It Mean to Be "Transactional"?

Being transactional means all of the following:

1. Understanding, accepting, and even embracing management as a day-to-day negotiation

2. Embracing the fact that everything that is not a deal-breaker is open to negotiation

3. Tying financial rewards and detriments only to measurable instances of employee performance

4. Also tying nonfinancial rewards and detriments to employee performance

5. Using each employee's unique needs and wants to make custom deals

6. Having the discipline and guts to enforce every deal that you make

Again, let's take a closer look.

1. Understanding, Accepting, and Even Embracing Management as a Day-to-Day Negotiation

This is the new reality of managing people. Accepting it means abandoning the top-down assumptions of hierarchical leadership and letting go of insult when direct reports resist your authority and make demands. It means constantly answering the questions that are always on every employee's mind: "What's the deal around here? What do you want from me? And what do I get for my hard work—today?"

Does that mean that everything is open to negotiation? Of course not. In fact, to become a transactional manager, the first thing you have to do is decide what is not negotiable. What are the basic performance standards, that is, the standards for which employees should expect nothing more than to be treated fairly, paid for their work, and keep their jobs? Those are your deal-breakers. Whatever they are, you have to figure it out and then be very clear: "OK. Here's the deal." That becomes your starting point.

Just remember that you'll have to remind people of that basic "deal" on a regular basis. And be aware that the more deal-breakers you start with—that is, the fewer items that are negotiable—the fewer bargaining chips you'll have at your disposal to drive performance.

2. Embracing the Fact That Everything That Is Not a Deal-Breaker Is Open to Negotiation

Don't be alarmed by the idea of negotiation. Many of your employees are probably negotiating with you already on a regular basis. It's only a problem if you are not negotiating back.

This means you have to be prepared to negotiate and get really good at it, taking control of the dynamic and using the ongoing negotiation to drive performance. Let's say you want an employee to be ambitious about achieving a particular set of goals by a particular deadline. How do you know what's fair? What's reasonable? You find out by negotiating. Let market forces decide. See what negotiation yields. For example, an exchange between you and a direct report might go like this:

> *You:* "I need you to do [x, y, z] by Thursday at 2 p.m. Do you understand? Can you do that?"
>
> *Report:* "But that's too much. That will take me until Friday afternoon."
>
> *You:* "I think you can do it by Thursday at 2 p.m."

Report: "Maybe by Friday morning."

   You: "How about the end of the day Thursday?"

Report: "OK."

And there you have a done deal. You would just have to be hands-on enough to hold that person accountable and enforce the deal.

3. Tying Financial Rewards and Detriments Only to Measurable Instances of Employee Performance

What if the compensation system in your organization doesn't allow you to do this? Then you have to do what you can within the limitations of the system. My experience has taught me that most compensation systems allow managers to use much more discretion than they actually use.

There are often opportunities to distinguish between and among employees on the basis of performance in ways that directly affect their compensation. Depending on the situation, this can mean any of a number of things, such as:

- Having the guts to give high-level performers higher scores and lower-level performers lower scores in project evaluations and in semi-annual and annual reviews

- Working with limited bonus pools and allocating funds among team members according to performance, rather than evenly across the board

- Using limited spot-bonus funds to reward some higher-level performers

- Having to go to bat to get additional discretion or additional funds so that you can, in fact, reward the performers who deserve to be rewarded

In every case, if you are going to have the guts to distinguish between team members on the basis of performance and put your money where your mouth is, you had better make sure you have been hands-on every step of the way.

To succeed, you must do these three things:

- Give every individual a chance to set and meet ambitious goals and deadlines on a regular basis.

- Keep an accurate ongoing analysis of each individual's performance.

- Document everything clearly and consistently in writing.

4. Also Tying Nonfinancial Rewards and Detriments to Employee Performance

Does this mean you tie every nonfinancial reward to performance? What about shared rewards, such as use of the company gym, attendance at the company picnic, or something as basic as tools and workspace? And what about shared detriments, such as cost-cuts that affect everyone equally?

It is true that in most organizations, shared rewards and detriments are often allocated without regard to individual performance. And it is true that these do contribute to important business goals like employee wellness, corporate culture, overall morale, and feelings of belonging. But unless you want to run a club instead of a business, you should make as many rewards and detriments as you possibly can purely contingent on measurable individual performance. Remember, these are your "bargaining chips" for negotiating increased performance, and the key is to gain control of as many of them as possible.

This means you often have to be creative and use the discretion and discretionary resources at your disposal. Use your power over such things as:

- Resources and work conditions
- The assignment of tasks
- Training opportunities
- Scheduling
- Recognition
- Exposure to decision-makers
- Work locations and work partners

In my view, if you have a candy jar on your desk and a direct report reaches for a piece of candy, you should stop that person in his or her tracks and say, "So, you want a treat? Well, here's what I need from you . . . by

this deadline . . . and here are the guidelines . . . Do
you understand?"

5. Using Each Employee's Unique Needs and Wants to Make Custom Deals

Every employee has at least one "needle in a haystack"
—a unique need or want. Look for these "needles" in
your individual performers and use them to make custom deals in exchange for exceptional performance.

In any workplace, you'll find a broad range of these so-
called needles: One person wants Thursdays off, while
another wants Mondays; one person wants to bring her
dog to work, while another wants to bring his house-
plants; one person wants to work with Sam and never
Chris, while another wants to work with Chris and
never Sam; and so forth. As simple as it may seem,
such needs and wants can be particularly powerful bargaining chips. Thus it is important to identify as many
as you can and use them to the fullest extent possible.
Also, keep in mind that an individual may have more
than one needle for you to find in "the haystack."

Look for something the employee really needs or wants
and would probably be willing to do a lot to get—such
as work longer, harder, smarter, faster, or better. If you
can find a way to offer the individual that needle, then
you are in a position to make a custom deal. (As a
matter of note, this is what economists call "a unique
value proposition" because a person's unique needs

and wants will always be of more personal worth than their market value. It's a great way to do business—a win-win transaction.)

When you need extra leverage with, and extra mileage from, an employee, there is no better motivational tactic than using that person's needle in a haystack as a bargaining chip. That's why I always tell managers, "When your employees make unreasonable demands, don't be insulted, be grateful: They're telling you exactly what they want—handing you that needle in a haystack. It's much harder when you have to go looking for it."

Now, of course you cannot do everything for everybody. What you need in order to meet certain wants and needs may simply be unavailable. At such times, you have to tell the direct report, "I just can't do that. What you want isn't possible. But maybe I can do this instead." Although not ideal, this is better than saying, "There's nothing I can do for you."

Before turning someone down, be sure that indeed you cannot strike the bargain: We've learned from experience that when managers really put their creativity and energy to work, they usually can do more than they ever would have guessed. If you're willing to jump through hoops, bend over backward, and go to bat for what you need, you'll find you can often get the resources you need and be able to make special deals with direct reports that you never thought possible.

6. Having the Discipline and Guts to Enforce Every Deal That You Make

You must be prepared to enforce every deal you make, whether it's for increased financial rewards, nonfinancial rewards, or needles in a haystack. No deals should be permanent. Every deal should be on the table all the time, contingent on the direct report making good on his or her commitments to you. When your direct reports deliver for you, you deliver for them. If they fail to meet commitments, you must call them on that failure immediately and withhold the quid pro quo.

Don't be afraid to reward some people more than others. That's not unfair. Quite the opposite, it's the only fair way to do business. Give every person the chance to succeed, the chance to meet the basic expectations and then exceed them, and the chance to be rewarded in direct proportion to his or her performance.

Keep no secrets. Create trust and confidence through open communication and transparency. Every person should know exactly what you expect every step of the way and exactly what he or she must do to earn rewards, no matter how great or small those rewards might be. But never forget: If you're going to enforce those deals, you must be hands-on. You have to keep close track, monitoring and measuring every person's performance and documenting it in writing. Then don't flinch when it comes to delivering on your end of the bargain, whether rewards or detriments are due.

Get HOT: Be Hands-On and Transactional

The following guidelines will help get you on course to becoming a HOT manager.

- Become highly knowledgeable about the tasks and responsibilities of your direct reports.

- Start spending time with every direct report in daily coaching sessions.

- Use your coaching time with direct reports to talk about the work they are doing. Be sure to focus on performance standards and concrete assignments—that means talking about clear goals and deadlines.

- Provide direction, guidance, and support on a regular basis.

- Start a written tracking system so that you can monitor and measure every individual's performance on a daily basis. This will help you reward success and address failure.

- Understand, accept, and embrace the new reality that managing people has become a day-to-day negotiation.

- Embrace the fact that everything that is not a deal-breaker is open to negotiation. Decide what your deal-breakers are—what's not open to negotiation—and then be prepared to negotiate regularly about everything else.

- Whenever possible, tie financial rewards and detriments to measurable instances of employee performance and to nothing else.

- Be creative with your discretion and use your discretionary resources to tie nonfinancial rewards, incentives, and benefits to measurable instances of employee performance.

- Look for every employee's "needle in a haystack" and use it to make custom deals with individuals in exchange for exceptional performance.

- Have the discipline and guts to enforce every deal you make, and don't flinch when it comes to providing the promised rewards and detriments.

- And don't forget: *You cannot be hands-on without being transactional, and you cannot be transactional without being hands-on.*

2

Not So HOT . . .

OFTEN MANAGERS become defensive when they hear about HOT Management. Some say: "Why should I be hands-on? I have my own style. I'm hands-off. I believe in empowerment. I let my direct reports do things their way. They only hear from me if something goes wrong." Others say: "Why should I be transactional? My direct reports get paid to do their job. They should just do as they're told. I shouldn't have to negotiate with them. And I shouldn't have to offer them special incentives to achieve high performance." These viewpoints may be perfectly reasonable. However, they are out of touch with the new realities of the workplace. Ultimately, the role of a supervisory manager is to drive performance. And the old ways simply don't work very well any more.

Being Hands-Off: The Problem

The old "hands-off" approach may seem fine in theory, but the most effective managers in today's workplace know that it has many drawbacks in practice. If you are hands-off instead of hands-on, then . . .

- You are not informed about the details of your direct reports' tasks and responsibilities.

- You talk to direct reports about everything under the sun, but you don't talk with them enough about the work; as a result, you fail to provide them with regular direction and support.

- You are not positioned to help direct reports identify resource needs and meet those needs.

- You are not positioned to anticipate problems, help direct reports avoid problems, and help solve problems when they occur.

- You are unable to judge what expectations are reasonable.

- You are not involved enough to set ambitious, but still meaningful, goals and deadlines.

- You have a difficult time accurately assessing the appropriate scope of responsibility to delegate to direct reports.

- You are not in a position of power because your direct reports know you are out of the loop.

- You miss numerous routine opportunities to provide direct reports with on-the-job training and coaching.

- Problems that could be easily avoided get started.

- Problems that could be solved with relative ease get out of control.

- Resources are often squandered unnecessarily.

- Direct reports often misunderstand expectations and performance standards, as well as goals and deadlines.

- Direct reports sometimes go in the wrong direction on projects for days or weeks before anybody notices.

- You spend more time putting out fires because you haven't spent enough time preventing them.

- You spend more time on your own low-level tasks and responsibilities because you don't have the confidence to delegate them.

- You soft-pedal your authority until a serious problem occurs; then you let loose with an outburst of anger.

- You are not in a position to fairly and accurately monitor and measure success and failure.

- When it comes time to reward your high-level performers, you typically lack the documentation that would make it easy to justify the rewards.

- When it comes time to deal with your low-level performers, you typically lack the documentation that would make it easy to impose detriments or enforce removal.

Being Hierarchical: The Problem

The most effective managers in today's workplace also know that being hierarchical is simply outmoded. If you insist on being hierarchical, rather than becoming transactional, then . . .

- You will often be confused and frustrated by the new reality that managing people has become a day-to-day negotiation.

- You will fail to answer the questions that are always on every employee's mind: "What's the deal around here? What do you want from me? And what do I get for my hard work—today?"

- You will risk becoming a passive negotiator, and unwittingly falling on the losing end, as direct reports pursue negotiations with you anyway, bargaining on a range of issues on a regular basis.

- You will find a growing disconnect between your management style and the needs, expectations, and behaviors of an increasing percentage of your employees.

- You will not be in a position to take control of the ongoing negotiation to drive performance.

- You will be unable to use market forces (negotiation) to collaborate with direct reports on what performance expectations are reasonable; thus you will be unable to make direct reports actively agree to ambitious goals and deadlines.

- Your direct reports will not feel the self-imposed source of accountability that comes from actively negotiating and agreeing to ambitious goals and deadlines.

- You will not be in a good position to tie financial and nonfinancial rewards and detriments to measurable instances of employee performance and nothing else.

- Efforts to implement "pay for performance" will fail because the tactic only works if people know exactly what behavior is required to merit rewards. That clarity comes from ongoing negotiation between direct reports and supervisors.

- Your direct reports will often receive the same rewards, regardless of individual performance levels and efforts. That is profoundly unfair, and a real motivation killer.

- Because direct reports see no direct connection between performance and rewards, they will be much less willing to make short-term sacrifices and go the extra mile.

- You will not be in the position to identify the "needle(s) in a haystack" of each direct report and to use those unique needs and wants to create "unique value propositions."

- You will deprive yourself of the extra leverage that comes from using a person's needle in a haystack as a bargaining chip.

- You will be less likely to monitor and measure performance closely, because you won't have to.

- Many of your direct reports will have unmet needs and wants—and no reasonable expectation of changing that situation through their own efforts.

- High-level performers will likely leave for work-places where they can reap rewards in proportion to their merit; low-level and mediocre performers will likely stay, being comfortable in a workplace that is not performance-based.

- You will attract and hire more and more low-level and mediocre performers, and fewer and fewer outstanding ones.

Accepting the New HOT Reality

The bottom line is, managers cannot get away with being hands-off and hierarchical anymore. The costs are far too high. If you are a hands-off supervisor, you are just not doing your job. And if you are still trying to be top down, figuring people will work like crazy based on vague promises of long-term rewards, then you are operating in fantasyland.

Being hands-on and transactional is high maintenance. It may be an insult to your position in the hierarchy, and it might make you feel like your authority is not sufficiently respected, but so what. You are not running a kingdom. You are running a business. Your job is to maximize return on investment, drive productivity and quality, and ensure good work is getting done at a good pace all day long. That means you have to do what works. Don't tell me that you have your "own style" of managing and are reluctant to change it—that's like saying you have your "own style" of accounting and are loathe to adopt the general ledger system. What works is not a personal affront to be defensive about. It is simply *what works*.

The world is changing. The workforce is changing. And by the way, other employers are changing. If you don't change, you'll be obsolete before you know it. So accept the new reality. You may end up actually liking it.

3

Reality Check:
Are You and Your Team Ready to Be HOT?

BEFORE WE PROCEED further with the nuts and bolts of HOT Management, a reality check is in order. This chapter provides that reality check in the form of three self-assessments and two team assessments. They will help you exercise your thinking and determine your readiness for the HOT approach.

About the Self-Assessments

For most managers, HOT Management takes a real adjustment in mindset. But that's not all. It also takes guts, determination, skill, consistency, a whole new set of habits, and time.

- Are you ready to muster all those resources?
- How far must you go from where you are today?
- Do you have a good sense of how much change you will have to make in order to start practicing the techniques of HOT Management?

- What obstacles stand in the way of your being a HOT manager?

The self-assessments will help you clarify these important issues.

About the Team Assessments

Once you've completed the self-assessments, you need to figure out how far your team has to go. Being managed by a HOT manager is extremely rewarding, but it is also extremely demanding. And being part of a HOT team is intense.

- Is your team ready to commit to high performance and nothing else?

- Which of your direct reports are already high-level performers who are likely to adapt well to HOT Management?

- Which of your direct reports will require a substantial adjustment?

- Which direct reports are mediocre or low-level performers?

- Are you currently familiar with the tasks and responsibilities of each individual, or will you have to spend some time getting up to speed?

- What are the key performance issues you'll have to focus on with each individual?

- What are the key incentives you'll want to use to motivate each individual?

The team assessments that round out this chapter will help you clarify those essential issues.

Be sure to consult your completed team assessments as you read the rest of this book. Remember: HOT Management is about your relationship with these individuals. It is your responsibility to help every person work harder, smarter, faster, and better.

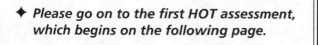

✦ *Please go on to the first HOT assessment, which begins on the following page.*

HOT ASSESSMENT 3A — SELF
What Are the Obstacles?

Directions: Identify and assess your obstacles to HOT Management by answering the questions below.

1. Think about what it will take for you to implement HOT Management:

   • What obstacles will you face from red tape and bureaucracy?

   • What obstacles will you face from your organization?

   • What obstacles will you face from your boss?

   • What obstacles will you face from your team?

➡

HOT ASSESSMENT 3A — CONCLUDED

- What obstacles will you face from yourself?

2. Next to each obstacle you've listed above, indicate whether or not that obstacle is within your control.

3. Again, look back at each obstacle you've listed above. Is the obstacle "100 percent"—so great that it will prevent you from implementing Hot Management at all? Or is it a partial limitation that will prevent you from achieving 100 percent implementation of HOT Management? Record your answer next to the obstacle.

HERE'S THE PUNCH LINE:

Of course there will be obstacles to HOT Management: This is the real world. Be honest with yourself about the things that are truly beyond your control. Realize they are simply not your concern anymore. Why should they be? You cannot control them! Take this approach:

1. Focus on what you can control. Be thorough and courageous and tackle those obstacles.

2. Be honest with yourself: there are no "100 percent" obstacles—I've learned that from experience.

3. Accept the fact that you won't be able to achieve a 100 percent implementation of HOT Management. If you can only achieve partial implementation, whether that be 20 percent or 50 percent or 90 percent, so what? There are no 100 percent solutions to anything. Deal with the obstacles. Work around them. Do as much as you can today. And try to do even more tomorrow.

HOT ASSESSMENT 3B — SELF
Do You Have the Guts and Skill?

Directions: Each HOT guideline is listed below along with a series of questions. Answer these questions to review your current management practice and to determine how ready and willing you are to commit to the HOT approach.

1. Become highly knowledgeable about the tasks and responsibilities of your direct reports.

   • What is my current practice? And why?

   • Do I currently have the skill to use this HOT technique effectively? If not, do I have the guts to practice this technique and develop the skill?

   • Will I commit to making this technique a habit?

2. Start spending time with every direct report in daily coaching sessions.

   • What is my current practice? And why?

   • Do I currently have the skill to use this HOT technique effectively? If not, do I have the guts to practice this technique and develop the skill?

   • Will I commit to making this technique a habit?

➥

HOT ASSESSMENT 3B — CONTINUED

3. Use your coaching time with direct reports to talk about the work they are doing. Focus on performance standards and concrete assignments—that means talking about clear goals and deadlines.

   - What is my current practice? And why?

   - Do I currently have the skill to use this HOT technique effectively? If not, do I have the guts to practice this technique and develop the skill?

   - Will I commit to making this technique a habit?

4. Provide regular direction, guidance, and support.

   - What is my current practice? And why?

   - Do I currently have the skill to use this HOT technique effectively? If not, do I have the guts to practice this technique and develop the skill?

   - Will I commit to making this technique a habit?

5. Start a written tracking system so that you can monitor and measure every individual's performance on a daily basis.

- What is my current practice? And why?

- Do I currently have the skill to use this HOT technique effectively? If not, do I have the guts to practice this technique and develop the skill?

- Will I commit to making this technique a habit?

6. Understand, accept, and embrace the new reality that managing people has become a day-to-day negotiation.

   - What is my current practice? And why?

   - Do I currently have the skill to use this HOT technique effectively? If not, do I have the guts to practice this technique and develop the skill?

   - Will I commit to making this technique a habit?

7. Embrace the fact that everything that is not a deal-breaker is open to negotiation. Decide what your deal-breakers are and then be prepared to negotiate regularly about everything else.

   - What is my current practice? And why?

➡

HOT ASSESSMENT 3B — CONTINUED

- Do I currently have the skill to use this HOT technique effectively? If not, do I have the guts to practice this technique and develop the skill?

- Will I commit to making this technique a habit?

8. Whenever possible, tie financial rewards and detriments to measurable instances of employee performance and to nothing else.
   - What is my current practice? And why?

   - Do I currently have the skill to use this HOT technique effectively? If not, do I have the guts to practice this technique and develop the skill?

   - Will I commit to making this technique a habit?

9. Be creative with your discretion and use discretionary resources to tie nonfinancial rewards, incentives, and benefits to measurable instances of employee performance.
   - What is my current practice? And why?

   - Do I currently have the skill to use this HOT technique effectively? If not, do I have the guts to practice this technique and develop the skill?

➥

- Will I commit to making this technique a habit?

10. Look for every employee's "needle in a haystack" and use those needles to make custom deals with individual performers in exchange for exceptional performance.

- What is my current practice? And why?

- Do I currently have the skill to use this HOT technique effectively? If not, do I have the guts to practice this technique and develop the skill?

- Will I commit to making this technique a habit?

11. Have the discipline and guts to enforce every deal you make, and don't flinch when it comes to providing the promised rewards and detriments.

- What is my current practice? And why?

- Do I currently have the skill to use this HOT technique effectively? If not, do I have the guts to practice this technique and develop the skill?

- Will I commit to making this technique a habit?

HOT ASSESSMENT 3C — SELF
How Much Time Will You Need?

Directions: The following will help you assess how much time you will need to begin practicing HOT Management. It will also get you started on developing strategies for making that time.

Remember: In an ideal world, you would devote a 15-minute coaching session *every day* to each person on your team; in the real world, you must commit to holding such sessions *at least once a week* with each person on your team.

1. How much time will be required to hold a 15-minute coaching session with each person on your team? To determine this, simply multiply the number of your direct reports by 15.

   - Number of Direct Reports:
   - Number [   ] x 15 = [   ] Minutes Needed

2. Begin thinking strategically.

   - How many coaching sessions a week, total, can you commit to?
   - How much time will that take?

   Again, you must commit to having a 15-minute session with every person at least once a week—more often is better, with every day being the best. Also keep in mind that every direct report is different (some will require more time than others), and that a person's time-needs can vary from week to week.

   Record your ideas below.

3. Figure out your time-management strategy. For example, exactly how will you dedicate the time?

   - One hour per day? If so, when? First thing in the morning, or in the afternoon?
   - A block of hours on a set day each week? If so, when?
   - Through scheduled appointments with each direct report (at least once a week)?
   - When will you schedule those appointments?
   - How will you make sure those appointments are not bumped?

   Record your ideas below.

4. Look ahead at your next full week. Can you work your time-management strategy into your schedule? Is it realistic? If not, start over. Record your modifications below.

HERE'S THE PUNCH LINE:

You absolutely must make the time if you are going to become a HOT manager.

HOT ASSESSMENT 3D - TEAM

Analyzing Your Team

Directions: List your direct reports below; then for each, answer the following questions:

- What is this person's performance level? High, mediocre, or low?
- Do you think this person has the potential to perform at a higher level?
- Will this person be one of the initial targets on whom you will focus intensively in the early stages of HOT Management?

DIRECT REPORT	PERFORMANCE LEVEL (High, Mediocre, Low)	POTENTIAL? (Yes/No)	INITIAL TARGET? (Yes/No)

HOT ASSESSMENT 3D — CONCLUDED

DIRECT REPORT	PERFORMANCE LEVEL (High, Mediocre, Low)	POTENTIAL? (Yes/No)	INITIAL TARGET? (Yes/No)

HOT ASSESSMENT 3E — TEAM
Analyze Each Team Member

Directions: Duplicate the sample form below and complete one for each
direct report. Refer to your findings from the previous team assessment
to answer the first three questions; then go on to consider special incentives, general performance issues, and tasks and responsibilities. (If
you have trouble with tasks and responsibilities, then you will know you
have to get up to snuff.)

Name of Direct Report:

1. Performance: Is this person's performance level high,
   mediocre, or low?

2. Potential: Does this person have the potential to improve
   performance?

3. Initial target: Is this person one of your initial HOT targets?

4. Special incentives: Has this person made special requests
   that you know of? If so, what are they? If not, do you have
   other information to draw on?

5. General performance issues: What key issues will you need
   to focus on with this person? What areas need work?

HOT ASSESSMENT 3E — CONCLUDED

6. Tasks and responsibilities: What are the specific tasks and responsibilities of this person? What are their related performance issues? What areas need work? Record your answers below.

TASKS AND RESPONSIBILITIES	PERFORMANCE ISSUE	AREA TO WORK ON

7. Adaptability: How well is this person likely to adapt to HOT Management?

4

Getting Started:
Introducing Your Team to HOT Management

BEFORE YOU MAKE A MAJOR SHIFT in your management style and start implementing HOT Management, you should prepare your team for the changes ahead. How are you going to do that?

1. Hold a team meeting to announce the change.
2. Hold an initial one-on-one meeting with each team member.

This is our recommended two-step approach.

The Team Meeting

Hold the meeting with your entire team. Make sure you go into it without any doubts about the changes you are about to propose, and that you are firmly intent on implementing HOT Management. Be prepared to deal with cynicism, as it's likely that at least some direct reports will think the HOT approach is just the management "flavor of the month"—a quick-fix idea you picked up from a book or seminar that will quickly get discarded. You will need to fully convince people that HOT is not some fly-by-night idea, but something you are going to start doing, something you are going to stick with, and something that is not going to go away.

Here is a suggested outline of what to say to your team:

- **Your Purpose:** "We're all under more pressure, with more expected of all of us. We have to find a way to work together to do more—faster, smarter, and better—but without additional resources. Let me tell you how I propose to do that: I'm going to try very hard to be a better manager. That's what this meeting is about.

  "I want you to know that I'm making a commitment to being a more effective manager. I'm going to require more from every person on the team. And I'm going to try to do more for every person on the team."

- **The Specifics:** "The number one thing I'm going to do is meet with every person on a regular basis. This will help me become more knowledgeable about every person's work so that I can be more engaged and more effective.

  "How often will we meet? It will be different for every person.

  "What will we discuss in our meetings? We'll discuss performance standards, concrete expectations, goals, deadlines, and guidelines. We will also discuss resource needs, troubleshooting, and ways that I can provide you with coaching and support. Essentially, we're going to talk about what I need from you—and what you need from me.

"I want you to know that I'm going to bend over backward to do more for this team. I will be asking a lot from every one of you, and I will try my best to do more for every one of you in return.

"I'm going to work to get more resources so that I can offer the rewards you want, but you need to understand that I will be looking very hard at performance. And I will do everything I possibly can to make sure that rewards on this team flow in direct proportion to performance, every step of the way."

- **Questions:** "Does everyone understand? Does anyone have any questions?"

Be prepared for your team to have many questions indeed. Typically, members wonder about such things as:

- How you plan to keep track of their work. Will you become a micro-manager?

- Why this is happening. Are they in trouble? Are their jobs in jeopardy?

- Whether this will affect their assignments, their work conditions, and their paychecks

- What kind of rewards are in it for them. Have you secured additional funds for bonuses?

- Whether you have the authority to make these changes. Have you checked this out with Human Resources? With Legal? With your boss?

- How you are going to measure their work and decide on rewards and detriments

Don't be surprised if the meeting turns into an intense discussion about the team's past, present, and future.

Again, be prepared for the meeting. Think through what you plan to say, and equip yourself with answers to the questions you are likely to face. Go into the meeting strong, confident, and ready to negotiate all these details and many more. Don't forget that some questions will be better answered in one-on-one meetings to come. And please remember, sometimes the best response is "I don't know yet. We'll have to see how it goes."

Initial One-on-One Meetings

Once you've had your team meeting, hold an initial meeting with each team member. The structure of these meetings is similar to that of the team meeting. Here is a suggested outline of what to say:

- **Purpose:** "As I told the entire team, I want to be a better manager. That's what this is about. We're all under more pressure, with more expected of all of us. I will try to do more for the team and more for every individual. But I'm going to require more from every individual."

- **Documentation:** "I'm going to keep a written record of our conversations, now and in the future. Do you understand that? Let me show you the format I will use. Does this make sense to you? Would you like me to provide you with a copy of the notes I take on our conversations?"

- **The Specifics:** "The number one thing I will do from now on is meet with YOU on a regular basis. How often should that be? Let's talk about it. [*Discuss issue.*]

"I want to become more knowledgeable about your work, so let's talk about the details of your tasks and responsibilities. I have the following questions about each task and responsibility." [*Ask the questions.*] What's on your plate right now? How long have you been working on it? How much longer will this be your main focus? Should we rethink this? Are there other things I should know?

"In our regular meetings, we'll discuss performance standards, concrete expectations, goals, deadlines, and guidelines. We'll also discuss resource needs, troubleshooting, and ways that I can provide you with coaching and support. In fact, let's talk about that right now. Here's what I need from you: [*Explain*]. What do you need from me?"

- **Questions:** "Do you understand? Do you have any questions?"

- **Scheduling Next Meeting:** "Let's decide when we will have our next meeting [*or initial coaching session*]."

Again, be prepared for lots of questions and concerns. Everyone will want to figure out exactly what HOT Management is going to mean for them on a personal level.

- Will they be doing more work, or less? (The answer is more!)

- Will they be under more scrutiny or less? (More!)

- Will they have more contact with you or less? (More!)

- Will they be working harder? (Sometimes. But they'll definitely be working smarter, faster, and better.)

- Will they have to put in more time? (Probably not. They'll spend less time putting out fires and more time achieving the mission.)

- Will they still have as much responsibility and freedom? (Exactly as much as they earn.)

- What's in it for them? (More guidance, support, and coaching from you!)

- What specific rewards are in it for them? (Exactly as much as they earn.)

Remember: In these initial meetings, you are presenting good news, not bad. You are committing yourself and your team to a management relationship that ensures high performance all the time. That's good for you as a manager, it's good for the team, and it's good for every member of the team. And you are going to make sure that rewards follow performance every step of the way. So this is a great opportunity for everyone to increase their financial and nonfinancial rewards by working with you to eliminate waste, avoid problems, and focus on achieving valuable results.

5

The Key to HOT Management:
Daily Coaching Sessions

THE KEY PRACTICE and centerpiece of HOT Management is the regular coaching session. Once again, ideally this would be a daily session with each direct report; at the very minimum, it must be a weekly session with each direct report.

Why the Coaching Sessions Are So Important

These regular meeting are essential for many reasons:

- Preparing for them forces you and your direct report to remain up-to-speed and up-to-date about the key details of the direct report's tasks and responsibilities. When managers stay in the loop, everybody stays clear and thoughtful.

- They will allow you to monitor changes in each direct report's workload, pace, level of difficulty, and corresponding needs.

- They will let you know when you need to step up guidance and support, and when you can back off. You'll thus be able to apply the right amount of pressure to keep each person focused on ambitious goals and deadlines.

- They will put you in a great position to troubleshoot, to bring in additional resources, and to change direction when necessary.

- They will help you measure success and failure and steer rewards to the right people at the right times.

But that is not all. Perhaps the most important thing about regular coaching sessions is the very act of making time several times a week to discuss expectations. This is a tremendous source of psychological accountability and the key to practical accountability. When managers and direct reports talk regularly about the details of the work to be done, the relationship takes on a new focus: It becomes a partnership of shared expectations for high performance.

We talk about the work every day because we want to review the overall performance standards and the very clear expectations for today, tomorrow, and next week. "Here's what I need from you. What do you need from me? Do you understand?" When a manager's relationship with direct reports takes on this new focus, the whole workplace is transformed: It's all about the work. That's what we're doing here together. Working!

The coaching session is also a chance to check in and make sure there is nothing in the way of performance, nothing in the way of getting lots of work done very well and very fast, all day long. There are so many questions every single day:

- Are there problems that need to be spotted?
- Problems that need to be solved?
- Resource needs that must be identified?
- Resources that must be gathered?
- Is there anything that's not clear?

The regular coaching session is a chance to get those questions out of the way and get on with the work.

Of course, it's also a chance for managers to engage in important reminders, to teach, to test the knowledge and preparedness of direct reports, to make sure direct reports are on board and engaged, and to generate some urgency. But most of all, again, it is the key to accountability. It's a lot harder, mentally and physically, for a direct report to fail if you talk about expectations up front, spelling out goals and deadlines, and everyone says, "Yes. I understand. I can do that."

So this is the most important habit to develop: Schedule and carry out a regular meeting with every direct report every day (or every other day or once a week). You have to make the time. You have to create the habit.

The Daily Coaching Session

Every conversation with a direct report will vary, but there are some basics that should remain consistent. Your regular meetings should follow this general format:

1. **Ask about changes:** "Has anything happened since our last meeting that I should know about?"

2. **Review progress and ask for an update:** "Let's review the progress you have made since our last meeting. Last time we talked about [*subjects discussed*]." Subjects will likely include some or all of the following:
   - Performance standards
   - Goals, guidelines, and deadlines
   - A specific to-do list
   - Resource needs
   - Troubleshooting
   - What the direct report needs from you

   Ask the direct report, "Could you please give me a progress report on each of these areas?"

3. **Provide evaluation and feedback:** "OK, here is my evaluation and feedback on those areas."

4. **Provide direction:** "Here's what I want you to do next." This will likely include some or all of the following:
   - Performance standards
   - Goals, guidelines, and deadlines

- A specific to-do list
- Resource needs
- Troubleshooting
- What the direct report needs from you

5. **Check for clarity:** "Do you understand? Is that fair?"

6. **Ask about needs:** "Is there anything that you need from me?"

In following the above format, keep in mind that every individual is different and work is a moving target. You must take charge and offer clear direction on the basics: performance standards, goals, deadlines, guidelines, and parameters.

You must also encourage input from your direct reports throughout the process. Talk through the basics, and work together:

- Try to reach agreement on what is reasonable.
- Think about problems that might develop.
- Anticipate resource needs.
- Strategize on how to reach ambitious targets.

Give your direct reports some ownership and complicity in the goal-setting process. And be prepared to negotiate every step of the way (using anything that isn't one of your deal-breakers).

✦ Assignment, Assessment, and Accountability

We call the HOT coaching session a "triple-A meeting." "Triple A" stands for assignment, assessment, and accountability.

Assignment. For every assignment, be sure to spell out the guidelines for acceptable performance and to reach mutual agreement on measurable goals and deadlines. Help your people think through each assignment at the outset by identifying resource needs, anticipating problems that may arise, and strategizing on obstacles to be hurdled.

You should also keep good track of every assignment and be available to coach employees through any problems that arise.

Assessment. Each assignment leads to an assessment, which leads to a new or modified assignment. Clearly, this involves keeping track of many details. Whatever method you choose, keep written records of your meetings with each person.

Don't keep your assessments a secret: Give people feedback on their performance. Ask yourself: What does this person need to hear (rather than want to hear)? If someone's performance starts to slip, call that person on it immediately and clarify expectations; then provide feedback to get the person back on track. Be kind, but have the guts to be honest. You serve no one if you hedge on or delay constructive feedback.

Accountability. It's important to put the locus of control for success in the employee's own hands as much as possible. As you delegate assignments, get each person to commit to measurable goals and deadlines every step of the way. This means seeking input on reasonable goals and deadlines as well as negotiating more ambitious ones. This sense of ownership empowers people because it puts success or failure within their own control.

✦ HOT QUESTION: *What Do You Do Between Meetings?*

Between meetings, it is critical to let direct reports "own" their goals and deadlines. This means not intervening in their work until your next meeting or until they request more input from you.

Tailoring the Sessions

Some direct reports work on the same tasks and responsibilities every day, whereas others work on different projects from one day to the next. How will you be able to orient each coaching session to each person? For guidance, you'll have to depend on your growing knowledge of each direct report, his or her tasks and responsibilities, and the overall situation. And you'll have to be the judge of exactly what to focus on and what to say. The more hands-on you become, the stronger and more informed your judgments will be about what can be done and what cannot, what resources are necessary, what problems may occur, what expectations are reasonable, what goals and deadlines are sufficiently ambitious, and what counts as a genuine success.

Keeping Track and Staying Focused

Make sure that over time you do the following:

- Keep track of the frequency and length of meetings.
- Stay focused on the work itself.

✦ **HOT TIP:** *Review the Circle of Empowerment*

Earlier we saw that you can "empower" your direct reports by defining the terrain in which they have power. That terrain consists of effectively delegated goals with clear guidelines and concrete deadlines. You may find it helpful to review this information when preparing for your coaching sessions and determining how often to meet. See "The Question of Micro-Management Versus Empowerment" in Chapter 1.

Keep Track of the Frequency and Length of Meetings

Let me emphasize once again: In an ideal world, you would have a 15-minute session with every direct report every day; in the real world, you must hold a brief session with every direct report at least once a week. If you are sufficiently hands-on, you should be able to gauge how much time to spend with each direct report, depending on the person's tasks, responsibilities, and projects.

Stay Focused on the Work Itself

Don't let meetings turn into convoluted negotiations or protracted therapy sessions. Stay focused on the work and keep your language brief, straight, and simple.

Your most important task is to clarify daily (or weekly) goals and deadlines. You must articulate guidelines and parameters. Remember, your "meeting mantra" should be "Here's what I need you to do . . . by this day and time . . . and here are the guidelines . . . Do you understand?"

By staying acutely focused in this way, you will be prepared to evaluate performance on an ongoing basis and to provide the necessary advice, support, motivation, inspiration—and special rewards.

Don't Forget Negotiation

Your sessions are your prime opportunities to answer those questions that are always on every employee's mind: "What's the deal around here? What do you want from me? And what do I get for my hard work—today?" Remind direct reports of your deal-breakers, whatever they may be: "OK. Here's the deal." Be ready to negotiate everything else, but have the guts to make performance the basis for financial and nonfinancial rewards of every type (including those "needles in a haystack").

Give everyone the chance to succeed, the chance to meet the basic expectations and then exceed them, and the chance to be rewarded in direct proportion to personal performance.

✦ *The following worksheet will help you prepare for your daily coaching sessions.*

HOT WORKSHEET 5A
Preparing for Your Coaching Sessions

Directions: Duplicate the sample form below so that you have one for each direct report. Use the form to prepare for the session. As you work through it, check off the items that pertain to your discussion.

Note: In practice, you should first review your notes from the previous session and clarify your purpose for the session at hand. Then, until you are thoroughly familiar with HOT Management, use the basic agenda below to stay focused.

Direct Report:
Date:

1. Has anything happened since our last meeting that I should know about?

2. Let's review the progress you have made since our last meeting. The last time, we talked about . . .

   ❐ Performance standards
   ❐ Goals, guidelines, and deadlines
   ❐ A specific to-do list
   ❐ Resource needs
   ❐ Troubleshooting
   ❐ What you need from me
   ❐ Other

   Please give me a progress report on each of these areas.

3. OK, here is my evaluation and feedback on . . .

   ❐ Performance standards
   ❐ Goals, guidelines, and deadlines

➡

HOT WORKSHEET 5A — CONCLUDED

- ❐ A specific to-do list
- ❐ Resource needs
- ❐ Troubleshooting
- ❐ What you need from me
- ❐ Other

4. Here's what I want you to do next on . . .
    - ❐ Performance standards
    - ❐ Goals, guidelines, and deadlines
    - ❐ A specific to-do list
    - ❐ Resource needs
    - ❐ Troubleshooting
    - ❐ What you need from me
    - ❐ Other

5. Do you understand? Is that fair?

6. Is there anything you need from me?

NOTES:

Keeping Track:
The Manager's Notebook

AFTER THE DAILY COACHING SESSION, the most important discipline of HOT Management is documentation. I don't care what you call it—note taking, performance tracking, record keeping—or if you simply see it as creating a paper trail. The bottom line is, you must make an absolute habit of taking written notes of each coaching session with each direct report.

The Importance of Keeping Notes

Why is it so crucial for you to keep written notes of your daily coaching sessions? Because notes help you do the following:

1. Keep track of the details
2. Keep expectations clear
3. Create psychological accountability
4. Prove work accountability in the case of informal disputes

5. Create solid documentation in the case of formal disputes

Let's take a look at these five areas.

1. Notes Help You Keep Track of the Details

Even if you have just one direct report working a regular schedule, it takes a lot of brain-space to remember everything you've discussed in each coaching session. Assuming you have several direct reports, you simply must keep a written record. You can refer to this running log before each session to help you focus your questions, your evaluation of work in progress, your feedback, and your guidance on next steps.

2. Notes Help You Keep Expectations Clear

It's one thing to talk about performance standards, goals, guidelines, and deadlines; it's another thing for everyone to get the same message. Create clarity around expectations, and avoid misunderstandings, by writing down the essence of each discussion and then asking your direct report to look closely at your notes with you. The visual data will support the verbal data, better ensuring shared meaning and clear communication.

This advantage of note taking elevates the question "Do you understand?" to a higher level of certainty, for you can add to it: "This is what I'm writing down. Take a look. Is this your understanding too?"

3. Notes Help You Create Psychological Accountability

When you say something and then write it down, you are preserving what was said in the form of a tangible piece of evidence. Even when there is no legal significance to such documentation, there is an important psychological impact. Both parties know that the document can be referred to later and that it will trump any one person's memory. Direct reports are thus more likely to live up to their agreements, for if they don't, there will be no excuses or disputes to hide behind—and such exposure is embarrassing, at the very least. Direct reports also can feel more assured that you will live up to your agreements, for accountability works both ways, and such assurance can be highly motivating.

4. Notes Help You Prove Accountability in the Case of Informal Disputes

Documentation, as tangible evidence of work accountability, gives you solid support in the case of informal disputes. Sometimes you and a direct report may disagree on what was said about what and when. Again, the written record trumps disparate recollections.

Such documentation is also useful for justifying your selection of who receives special awards and who receives detriments. You can simply point to performance as the reason and offer your documentation as proof of performance.

5. Notes Help You Create Solid Documentation in the Case of Formal Disputes

Written notes are critical supports if you are faced with a formal dispute about your management of direct reports. Whatever the accusation or complaint, the people in Human Resources and Legal will want to know "what's in the file." You should be able to tell them that you have a detailed contemporaneous record of all your regular meetings with direct reports. That record—with its detailed documentation of performance standards, expectations, goals, deadlines, guidelines, resource needs, troubleshooting, and other special issues—will provide you with a paper trail to support your version of the facts.

You are always on safe legal ground as long as you give every person the same opportunity to succeed, make measurable performance of tasks and responsibilities the *only* factor in determining rewards and detriments, and keep notes to prove that you have followed those management practices.

The Manager's Notebook and What You Should Record in It

The best approach to documenting your sessions is to organize and keep a "manager's notebook." Use it for your running notes about your management relationship with each direct report. Keep in mind that you don't have to write a book—just keep a running log of your routine coaching sessions (and any special sessions) with every direct report.

Organize the notebook as a tracking system, both chronologically and by person. Then keep track of the essential details of your discussions about these topics:

- Overall performance standards
- Goals, deadlines, guidelines, and parameters
- Anticipating and planning for resource needs
- Anticipating and planning to avoid problems
- Questions asked by your direct report
- Requests made by your direct report
- Any quid pro quo you have promised in exchange for specific performance
- Any other special issues that come up

Using the Manager's Notebook

Managers often have similar questions about how to use their notebooks. Here are the most frequently asked questions and their answers:

- *When should I take notes?* You should refer to your ongoing log before every session with a direct report. At that time, jot down any notes that you need for the coaching session. Remember the basic meeting agenda (see page 60). Then make notes during the conversation as necessary.

- *Should I show my notes to the direct report?*
  While it is not always possible, practical, or
  necessary to do this, remember that by wrapping
  up a subject by showing your notes, you will gain
  more in terms of clear expectations, assignment
  reinforcement, and psychological accountability.
  You will also give the direct report an upfront
  opportunity to correct any misunderstandings.

- *Should I provide a copy of my notes to the
  direct report?* Again, this is not always possible,
  practical, or necessary. However, this practice
  can be especially useful with certain direct reports. If you decide to make a habit of it, you'll
  have to build in some process for getting copies
  to your direct reports.

- *Should I take notes after the session?* You
  should stop after every discussion, go over your
  notes, and make sure that you've recorded everything of consequence. If you remember something you want to add, write it down. Sometimes
  you'll think of something you want to mention in
  your next meeting with the person—in which
  case, write that down too.

Remember that the purpose of the manager's notebook
is to give you a working document that you can use as
an effective management tool. It should help you drive
performance, track performance, and stay on top of the
details of every direct report's tasks and responsibilities.

The Format of the Notebook

In terms of format, there are three possibilities:

1. A handwritten format using an old-fashioned ring binder and paper
2. An electronic format using computer software
3. A handwritten format using a bound notebook

Many managers prefer to keep their written notes in a binder. Others prefer to use scheduling/database software such as ACT, Lotus Notes, or Microsoft Outlook. If you are already working with this kind of software, then the electronic format is an excellent way to take an existing habit and modify it for use with HOT Management. Still other managers prefer a looser approach, and keep a diary-like notebook.

The format of your manager's notebook is your choice. Figure out which one will be the easiest for you to use, and then make an absolute habit of using it.

The Use of Standard Forms

You also need to decide what kind of form you will use for taking notes during the sessions. Typically, a standard fill-in-the-blank page will do. After the session, you can either add the page to your binder or install it in your software. Even if you prefer the diary-like approach to note taking, consider using some kind of form to keep notes organized (see "freestyle" form below).

It's likely that, ultimately, you'll want to create a form that is customized to meet your particular needs. For now, consider these three approaches (samples appear at the end of the chapter):

1. **Goals and Deadlines.** This is perhaps the most basic approach. Make a page with room at the top for the date, time, and direct report's name. Next, create four columns: Goals, Deadlines, Guidelines, and Comments. Be sure to leave room at the page bottom for a "Special Notes" section. Here are the user directions:

   • Log goals, deadlines, and guidelines as they are decided, using the appropriate spaces.

   • Record comments as they are made.

   • Use the "Special Notes" section to record discussion of such things as special projects, resource needs, anticipated problems, actual problems, uncertainties, special requests, and promised rewards.

   • When it is time to review progress, return to those columns and see if everything is on track.

2. **Tasks and Responsibilities Checklist.** This is a handy form to use if a direct report has a set list of daily tasks and responsibilities. Again, make a page with room at the top for the date, time, and direct report's name. Then make two columns. In the first, list all tasks and responsibilities, along

with check boxes; leave the second column blank for your comments. Be sure to include a "Special Notes" section. Here are the user directions:

- Check off items as you discuss them, and record comments beside them.

- Use the "Special Notes" section to record the discussion of such things as special projects, resource needs, anticipated problems, actual problems, uncertainties, special requests, and promised rewards.

- When it is time to review progress, simply work through the checklist and see if everything is on track.

3. **Freestyle.** If you prefer to keep a written diary, use some organizing principle for your notes. For instance, date each page as you go forward, and when you have a session with a direct report, write down his or her name. Label all pre-session notes "Before," all session notes "During," and all post-session notes "After." Always record the time of your "During" notes.

Consider using the sample form that has been provided for this approach. Its design and use are based on the suggestions above.

Whatever form you choose, don't forget that the idea is to create an approach that works easily for you so you can turn it into a habit.

MANAGER'S NOTEBOOK FORM — SAMPLE A
Goals and Deadlines

DATE and TIME:

NAME:

Goals	Deadlines	Guidelines	Comments

Special Notes:

MANAGER'S NOTEBOOK FORM — SAMPLE B
Tasks and Responsibilities Checklist

DATE and TIME:
NAME:

Tasks and Responsibilities	Comments
❏ 1.	
❏ 2.	
❏ 3.	
❏ 4.	
❏ 5.	
❏ 6.	
❏ 7.	
❏ 8.	
❏ 9.	
❏ 10.	

Special Notes:

MANAGER'S NOTEBOOK FORM — SAMPLE C
Freestyle

DATE and TIME:
NAME:

Before Session:

During Session (including time):

After Session:

Special Notes:

7

Doing More for People:
Using Bargaining Chips to Drive Performance

IF YOU WANT to be effective as a HOT manager, you must be able to put your money (and nonfinancial rewards) where your mouth is. You must be able to do more for your direct reports. We all know of managers who do more for their people. They bend over backward, jump through hoops, and go to bat to get more resources for their team. If you are not one of those managers, then what is your problem? The ability to do more for people is an important source of transactional power. It gives you a full rack of bargaining chips with which to drive performance.

The real trick with the bargaining-chip approach is to have the discipline to do more for your direct reports *only* when they do more for you. That is the art of the quid pro quo. "Here's what I need from you. What do you need from me?"

It is also important to realize that if you are going to commit to performance-based rewards—the essence of the bargaining-chip approach—you must do so properly. That means the following:

- Giving every direct report the opportunity to meet clearly defined expectations and thus earn performance-based rewards

- Spelling out, at the start, the performance required to earn those rewards

- Making sure the requirements are clear every step of the way

- Documenting the promises you and your direct report make to each other

- Monitoring the direct report's performance and measuring it against his or her promises

- Making every effort to deliver on your end of the deal

What Are Your Bargaining Chips?

Basically, there are two types of bargaining chips:

1. **Financial.** Here you need money for short-term cash bonuses. Examples include annual bonus pools, funds for spot bonuses, extra dollars on projects that run under budget, and special funds provided by request.

2. **Nonfinancial.** Here you need resources to use as short-term bonuses. Examples include days off, gift certificates, incentive trips, select parking,

learning opportunities, scheduling flexibility,
exposure to decision-makers, recognition (such
as "Employee of the Week"), and special items
such as mugs, t-shirts, and pens.

Do You Have the Power to Use Bargaining Chips?

Often when I discuss this issue with managers, they
claim to lack either the power to change the compensation system or the influence needed to make custom
deals with people. Based on my experience, I can tell
you this: You will never be able to do everything for
everyone, but you can almost always do more for almost
everyone. You just have to be willing to bend over backward and jump through hoops.

You will typically find that performance-based rewards
fall into one of these three categories:

- **Standard operating procedures.** An example of
  this would be sales commissions. If you have performance-based rewards already built into your
  system, make sure you know exactly how they
  work. See if you can make them work better as
  performance drivers by adjusting how you deploy
  them. Then think about how you discuss these
  rewards with direct reports. Start reminding your
  people about these rewards in your day-to-day
  conversations with them.

- **Rewards hidden within the system.** Often there are opportunities to reward performance with financial and nonfinancial resources, but they're hidden in the system and you must find them. Some companies have bonus pools or ranking systems that managers could use as performance-based options, but don't. Look for opportunities like this. When you find them, learn how to use them. And start bargaining with them for specific performance objectives with direct reports.

- **Resources to scavenge and hoard.** Most companies are filled with resources that go unmaximized except by those scavengers who know how to dig them up, gain control of them, and use them for their own purposes. Go out and unearth those resources and use them to drive performance.

The bottom line is, there's almost always a lot more you can do for people if you put your mind to it—whether it's making better use of standard operating procedures, finding opportunities hidden within the system, or digging up resources that are just waiting to be scavenged.

That said, it is also true that you won't be able to do everything for everybody. That's why, in your dealings with direct reports, you should always make three things clear:

- What is within your sphere of authority and influence—*"I can do that."*

- What may not be within your sphere of authority and influence—*"I can try to do that."*

- What is definitely not within your sphere of authority and influence, along with a substitute —*"I can't do that, but I can do this."*

In the latter case, see if you can provide a substitute that answers in some way to the direct report's need or want. For example, if you were managing a cashier in retail and that person asked to work as a telecommuter (an impossible request), you could try offering more scheduling flexibility.

Occasionally a requested reward is simply out of proportion to the performance in question. For instance, when asked to work late, a direct report might say, "Sure. For a thousand bucks." In such a case, you may have to reply, "Come on, that's ridiculous." But remember: Negotiation is always on. A counteroffer that *is* proportional might do the trick.

There are other times when a direct report's request might seem reasonable and appropriate, but you're not sure that you can make it happen. That's a good time to say, "I don't know if I can do it, but I will promise you this: I will go to bat for you." Even if that effort fails, it might very well be a valuable reward for your direct report just to know that you—a supervisor—are willing to work hard for your people when they work hard for you.

Getting Your Hands on More Bargaining Chips

By uncovering a whole menu of rewards for high performance, you will open up the terrain of possibilities for motivating your team. The more bargaining chips you have at your disposal, the more leverage you have to drive smarter, faster, and better performance. Here's my recommended three-step process:

1. Evaluate all the resources at your disposal under the current system. Often you will find there are opportunities within the present system to position rewards in exchange for performance.

2. Brainstorm ways to get discretionary resources under your control. Think about what you've done in the past. Think about what your colleagues have done. Think about what those managers who do more for their people are doing.

3. Try to position all rewards in exchange for performance. All requests made by direct reports should be considered only in relation to a quid pro quo of specific performance requirements. The same goes for any reward you consider giving to a direct report. And you should always consider offering a special reward when you are asking for performance above and beyond the norm. You must get in the habit of saying, "You want this? OK. Here's what I need from you. If you deliver for me, I'll do my best to deliver for you."

HOT EXERCISE 7A
Evaluate Your Current Resources

Directions: Evaluate your resources under the current system by answering the following questions. You may have to do some probing to answer question 2.

1. Are there performance-based rewards available to direct reports as a matter of standard operating procedure? If so, what are they?

   How do these rewards work?

   Who in the organization can advise you how to use them?

   How can you make better use of them?

2. Are there performance-based rewards hidden in the system? If so, what are they?

   How do these rewards work?

   Who in the organization can advise you how to use them?

   How can you make better use of them?

HOT EXERCISE 7B
Brainstorm Resources to Scavenge

Directions: Consider the following questions.

1. What extra resources do you know you could get your hands on?

2. What resources are now available but not being deployed as rewards for performance? Can you deploy some of those? How?

3. What are other managers doing? What resources are they getting their hands on?

➡

HOT EXERCISE 7B — CONCLUDED

4. Does your boss have any advice?

5. What about those outside your direct chain of command? Who else can you talk to about resources?

6. What about your direct reports? Do they have any ideas?

7. What can you learn from other companies?

THE KEY QUESTION:

Whatever resources you can get your hands on, remember the key question: How can you use those resources as bargaining chips to drive performance?

HOT WORKSHEET 7A
Use Bargaining Chips to Drive Performance

Directions: Use this sheet as a reference for your bargaining approach.

THE KEY: Try to position all rewards in exchange for performance. Get in the habit of telling direct reports: "You want this? OK. Here's what I need from you. If you deliver for me, I'll do my best to deliver for you."

1. Have ready your rack of bargaining chips.

2. Be prepared to hold a bargaining-chip negotiation in a positive, constructive way.

   A. Focus on team performance improvement. Explain that you are going to engage every team member in improving performance, and that in return you want to do more for each member.

   B. Present the bargaining-chip concept. Explain that you want to offer more rewards in exchange for performance. Let the direct report know that you have limited resources at your disposal and that you want to ensure those resources go to the people who are working longer, harder, smarter, faster, and better.

   C. Make sure the direct report understands that you cannot do everything for everyone, but will try to do more than what you're currently doing.

3. Explain that in your regular meetings, you will set ambitious goals and deadlines every step of the way, and that you want to be able to offer more rewards as incentives along the way.

4. Give the direct report some examples of the bargaining chips at your disposal. Ask which ones are of particular interest to the individual.

5. Discuss specific goals and deadlines. Then talk about going the extra mile. Set more ambitious goals and deadlines, and offer a bargaining chip as a reward for performance.

8

Custom Deals and "Needles in a Haystack"

IF YOU WANT to take the bargaining-chip approach one step further, then you are ready to make custom deals with your high-level performers. How? By finding and using "needles in a haystack," one person at a time, one day at a time.

Remember that "needles" are those unique needs and wants of individual direct reports. As we saw earlier, examples vary as much as people do and include such things as special schedules, working with some people instead of others, and bringing something personal (like a dog or a plant) to work. You must think about all the demands, even if some are unreasonable, and accept the fact that you cannot always meet every demand, including those that are reasonable.

Do your best, and always try to use custom deals to drive high performers to reach ever more ambitious levels of achievement.

Making Custom Deals for High Performance

In custom dealing, you simply take the bargaining-chip transactional approach one step further. When a direct report makes a special request or when you have a special request for a direct report, think about what that person wants or needs and determine whether you can offer a win-win transaction: "I'll do this for you, if you do [x, y, z] for me."

Special Arrangements

Custom deals often require that you make special arrangements. In most organizations, no matter what the rules are, special arrangements happen all the time. How do they happen? Someone makes them happen. That someone could be you.

Special arrangements sometimes require nobody's approval but your own. Other times, you do need to get approval, in which case the question is "From whom?" And, of course, there are some special arrangements that are simply prohibited—which means you'd better find out which ones so you can make it clear from the start that those are off the bargaining table.

Using "Needles in a Haystack"

Think about each direct report and try to identify his or her needles in a haystack. If you already know what the direct report wants or needs, the conversation is easy: "I want to discuss that special request you keep making. I might be able to do that for you, but here's what I need from you in exchange." If you don't know what the direct report wants or needs, you'll have to ask (and then make it clear what you need in return).

Once you have a "needles" list, run the requests by those whose approval you will need in order to grant the requests. Try to figure out which ones would be easy to grant, which ones would be difficult, and which ones might be impossible.

If you can't give a direct report exactly what he or she wants, then explain your limitations. Come as close as you can to granting the request. Zero in on the need that is being expressed, and work on a compromise to meet as much of that need as possible.

Accountability

When you have agreed on a deal, explain how you will hold the direct report accountable for his or her end of the bargain. Emphasize that you are willing to cater to personal needs, but only as long as the direct report consistently meets the goals and deadlines that both of you discuss in your regular meetings. If the person breaks his or her part of the bargain, it's off. If the person gets back on track, it's on again.

Making a custom deal with a direct report is an exceptional reward in itself; therefore, you should require exceptional performance in exchange. And it must be 100 percent clear that the deal is always on the table, contingent on continued high performance.

When Other Team Members Cry "No Fair!"

It would be challenging enough if you only had to negotiate a custom deal with the demanding, pain-in-the-neck super-achiever on your team. But the fact is, people are going to hear about the special deal you made with that person and then cry, "No fair! What about me?" The purpose of HOT Management is not to focus on one person, but to raise the performance bar for every member of your team. So don't even think about keeping custom deals a secret. In fact, put a billboard out in the parking lot that proclaims, "You want a custom deal? Come to my office and find out how to get one!"

When members come talk to you, focus on the "more for more" concept. Put the custom-deal idea in context, explaining where it fits into your new management approach. Remind them that in return for requiring more from every person, you are going to offer every person more. This is the "more for more" essence of HOT Management. Also explain the following:

- What a "custom deal" is and how it works.
  Give your team members some examples to get them thinking.

- That you will try hard to meet their needs, but may not be able to do so in all cases, all the time

- How each person is special, with special needs, and that the one-size-fits-all model of rewarding people just doesn't motivate people enough

- That you're ready to customize a great deal for each of them based on the great work they contribute, but that you'll need to take a much more hands-on approach to their work

- That you'll be meeting with them regularly to set and check in on goals, tasks, and responsibilities

At this point, assure members that the meetings will be focused, brief, and productive because you respect their time as much as you want them to respect yours. Also assure them that you will be providing more support and coaching for each person while holding them accountable for more ambitious goals and deadlines. You're not just going to demand more of them without giving them what they need to succeed.

Ensure that your team understands that any custom deals are contingent on consistently meeting goals and deadlines. Once they break their part of the bargain, the deal is off for that week (or that month—whatever you decide). When this happens, they'll get their deal back only when they prove to you that they're back on track and will remain on track consistently.

A Friendly Reminder

Be sure to remember: If you are going to commit to performance-based rewards, then you must keep to these guidelines:

- Give every person the opportunity to succeed against clearly defined expectations.

- Document the mutual promises.

- Monitor and measure the performance.

- Make every effort to deliver on your end of the deal.

HOT EXERCISE 8A
Brainstorm "Needles in a Haystack"

Directions: Answer the questions below. They will help you accept the fact that making custom deals can seem unreasonable. Do you have to use blackmail to drive performance? No. Just transactional power!

1. Think of the most unreasonable things that employees have ever asked you for. List as many as you can think of.

   Is there any way you could grant some of these requests? If so, what quid pro quo from the direct report would make it a good deal for you, the company, and the direct report?

2. Think of the most unreasonable things that you have ever asked for, or have never asked for because you thought they were too unreasonable.

   Is there any way you could grant some of these requests? If so, what quid pro quo from the direct report would make it a good deal for you, the company, and the direct report?

HOT EXERCISE 8B
Brainstorm Special Arrangements

Directions: Consider the following questions.

1. What special arrangements could you make available to your direct reports if you were willing to do the paperwork and monitor the arrangements? How would these arrangements work? The list below will help to get you thinking.

   • Flexible schedules:

   • Flexible location:

   • Flexible workspace set-up:

   • Special tasks, responsibilities, projects:

   • Special exposure to decision-makers:

   • Special learning opportunities:

   • Other:

2. What special arrangements have other managers made for direct reports? How do they work?

HOT EXERCISE 8B — CONCLUDED

3. What special arrangements do you know about in other organizations? How do they work?

4. Does your boss have any advice on this issue?

5. What about your direct reports? Do they have any ideas?

THE KEY QUESTION:

Whatever special arrangements you can make, keep in mind the key question: How can you use those arrangements to drive performance?

HOT EXERCISE 8C
Brainstorm Individual "Needles"

Directions: Think of one direct report at a time. For each one, ask yourself whether that person has made any unusual requests. Do you have some idea whether you can meet that person's wants or needs?

DIRECT REPORT	NEEDLES IN A HAYSTACK	LEVEL OF DIFFICULTY	WHO MUST APPROVE?

NEVER FORGET!

Granting a custom deal is an exceptional reward, so you should require exceptional performance in exchange. And it must be 100 percent clear that the deal is always on the table, contingent on continued high performance.

HOT WORKSHEET 8A

Preparing for the Custom-Deal Meeting

Directions: Let's say you have a high performer with whom you would like to make a custom deal. You want to do two things:

1. Reward that person for a good track record in performance.
2. Provide an incentive for that person to do more and to do it better, smarter, and faster.

Get ready for custom dealing with this person by responding to item 1. Then use the rest of the worksheet as a reference for your preparation.

---

1. Find the direct report's needle in a haystack:

- What flexibility has this person asked for in the past? Has he or she discussed this with you before? Is it something you think would motivate the person if you positioned it as a custom deal?

- What kind of flexibility would improve the direct report's work-life balance?

- What kind of workplace conditions would make this person's job more pleasant?

➡

- What kinds of things have motivated this person in the past?

Note: *If prior meetings have not clued you in on this person's "needle," then be ready to ask, listen, and keep an open mind during this meeting. Be aware that some people are reluctant to ask for what they need and thus do not reveal what will truly motivate them. You might have to draw them out with tailored, observant suggestions.*

2. Be prepared to hold a custom-deal negotiation in a positive, constructive way:

   A. Focus on the "more for more" concept. Explain that you are going to engage everyone on the team in improving his or her performance, and that in return you want to do more for each person.

   B. Explain the custom-deal concept, including how the custom deal works. Also explain that you want to negotiate a custom deal with this person because he or she has an exceptional track record so far and you want to provide rewards and additional incentives for continued exceptional performance.

   C. Explain that you cannot do everything for everyone, but will try to do more—especially for this person. Still, the deal will always be on the table, which means you'll be holding that person accountable for concrete goals and deadlines on an ongoing basis. Emphasize that you are going to push him or her to continue to achieve ambitious goals and deadlines in exchange for this custom deal.

   D. Explain that you will use your regular meetings to keep track of the custom deal.

9

High Performance—The Only Option:
Dealing With Performance Problems

YOU ALREADY KNOW that you will need to engage every direct report in regular coaching sessions to clarify expectations, to assign goals and deadlines, to assess performance, and to hold each person accountable every step of the way. But what do you do when, despite your regular coaching, a direct report fails to meet the performance standards and the daily goals and deadlines that the two of you have agreed on?

If you are practicing HOT techniques, then your management style will already be sending this message: "Our team is all about high performance. We talk about the work, in detail, every day. Then we get a lot of work done very well, very fast, all day long. High performance is the only option. There is no room for low performers on a HOT Team. And our team is 100 percent HOT." Performance failure thus means that you will have to proceed in a way consistent with the HOT approach.

The number one rule is, you cannot let people off the hook. Leniency with performance problems will diminish your credibility and undermine the team. If you don't deal with performance problems immediately and aggressively, then you will do a disservice to yourself, your team, and every person on the team.

The person you will let down the most, of course, is the direct report whose performance is failing. That person may wonder why you don't care enough to provide the help needed for success. And why would you let someone put his or her career in jeopardy? Why would you not help the person seize the opportunity to learn, grow, improve, and ultimately succeed?

Managing Performance Problems: The Five-Step Process

If a direct report's performance starts to slip, take immediate action by following these five steps:

1. Intensify your hands-on approach.
2. Diagnose the problem.
3. Prepare for a performance improvement intervention.
4. Script, rehearse, and conduct the intervention.
5. Be aggressive about follow-up.

Let's take a close look at each of these steps.

1. Intensify Your Hands-On Approach

Be even more hands-on for a while, narrowing the circle of empowerment:

- Step up your schedule of coaching sessions. Meet every day or even twice a day if necessary.

- Set smaller goals with shorter deadlines, and spell out even more guidelines and parameters for every goal.

- Be even more explicit about your expectations.

- Do what you must during each coaching session to ensure that the direct report completely understands. Always ask the person to explain his or her understanding of your expectations and the performance standards, goals, deadlines, and guidelines. Be sure to write this down in your manager's notebook; then show the direct report what you have written.

- Gain explicit verbal (and maybe even written) commitments with each coaching session.

- Provide more coaching, support, and guidance in between sessions. As you do this, pay close attention and gather as much information as you can. See if the problem improves. If it does, figure out how it's improving and why; if it doesn't, try to figure out what's going wrong and why.

2. Diagnose the Problem

If the first step does not result in improved performance, then you really have a performance problem on your hands and must diagnose it.

Nearly all performance problems fall into one or more of three categories:

- *Ability*
- *Skill*
- *Will*

If the problem is *ability,* then your direct report's natural strengths are simply not a good match with some or all of the tasks and responsibilities in his or her current role. In such a case, your best option is to change the tasks and responsibilities that are a poor match. If you cannot do that, you may have to remove the person from your team.

If the problem is *skill,* then the direct report does not have sufficient training for some or all of the tasks and responsibilities in his or her current role. In such a case, you'll need to find the skill gaps and ensure the person *immediately* receives the training needed to do the job. If you cannot do that, you may have to remove the person from your team.

If the problem is *will,* then the direct report has an internal or external issue that needs addressing. If the problem seems to be internal (depression, for example), then your best option may be to recommend therapy or some form of employee services. However, often problems of will are simply problems of external motivation. In such a case, you must explore incentives, to see whether there are any that will re-engage the person. If you cannot offer the necessary incentives or if, no matter what you offer, the problem continues, then you may have to remove the person from your team.

By analyzing performance problems in these terms—ability, skill, will—you should be able to move people quickly toward a solution.

3. Prepare for a Performance Improvement Intervention

Get ready to meet with the direct report and initiate a performance improvement intervention.

- **First, review your manager's notebook.** Think about your previous meetings with this person. What patterns of poor performance have you already documented? What measures, if any, have you already taken to correct the problem?

- **Second, clarify exactly what's wrong.** For example, does this person consistently fail to meet deadlines or goals? Does he or she fail to correct mistakes you've already discussed? Put your finger on the specific problem area or areas. If there is more than one area of performance to be improved,

you'll have to focus on one issue at a time.
So choose your first issue and "back-burner"
the others.

- **Third, identify specific examples of the problem area you've identified.** To prepare a good case, you'll need to gather evidence: pertinent details such as times, places, and projects where the employee failed to meet goals, make deadlines, and/or follow guidelines.

- **Fourth, review your initial analysis of the problem.** Decide if, with further thought, you would categorize the problem as one of ability, skill, or will.

- **Fifth, consider action steps.** Decide whether there are concrete action steps you are willing to take or are going to ask the direct report to take.

- **Sixth, before you proceed, consult an ally in Human Resources.** Make sure you are following proper procedures before you have your intervention conversation with the direct report. You want to make sure you are dotting your "i's" and crossing your "t's."

4. Script, Rehearse, and Conduct the Intervention

By creating and rehearsing a script for this difficult conversation, you will find it easier to stay on track during your meeting and more effectively address the direct report's arguments, excuses, and emotions.

As you prepare your script, think of the excuses the direct report typically offers for failing to meet deadlines or accomplish goals. Of course, some excuses are justifiable and can serve as springboards to discussing processes, parameters, or procedures that don't work any longer. But if you've been meeting with this person regularly, you've probably already sized up the legitimacy—or illegitimacy—of the excuses. The point is, you want to take a proactive approach to those excuses and address them before they are thrown at you again.

In your meeting, you'll need to do the following:

- **First, explain the meeting's purpose.** Make it clear that you are meeting to discuss a problem.

- **Second, remind the direct report that high performance is non-negotiable.** You'll need to confront the person in direct terms, stating that the failure to meet goals and deadlines is simply unacceptable.

- **Third, identify the performance problem.** Be as specific as you can, presenting the facts as you've documented them. Remember, you are evaluating the performance, not the person.

- **Fourth, talk about the problem in terms of ability, skill, and will.** Explain what each category means, and ask what the source of the problem might be. Offer your own insights if the person seems stuck or is off base in his or her analysis.

- **Fifth, agree on a plan to improve the performance problem.** Once you've reached agreement on the problem areas and their sources, discuss how the direct report and you can work together on those areas. Be sure the person understands that the only option is performance improvement.

- **Sixth, mention further coaching.** Explain that you will be working much more closely with the person to help turn the problem around and create an upward spiral of performance and rewards.

- **Seventh, sign a performance plan.** If you have put together a written performance improvement plan, then you and your direct report should both sign it and each walk away from the meeting with a copy.

Again: Before you do all this, make sure you have consulted an ally in HR to ensure you are following the proper procedures for your company.

5. Be Aggressive About Follow-Up

After the meeting, follow up aggressively and try to reverse the downward spiral. Intensify the hands-on approach, thus narrowing the circle of empowerment. Again, be sure to follow these guidelines:

- Hold frequent coaching sessions.

- Set relatively small goals with short deadlines, and spell out every guideline and parameter for every goal.

- Be very explicit about your expectations.

- Make sure that the direct report completely understands those expectations.

- Show the direct report what you are writing down in your manager's notebook.

- Gain explicit verbal commitments with each coaching session. If you think it would help, also get those commitments in writing.

- In between sessions, provide as much coaching, support, and guidance as you can.

As the direct report demonstrates improved performance, reduce your intensity, enlarging the circle of empowerment a bit at a time, until you reach a comfortable level of engagement.

What if there is no performance improvement? If the intervention fails, you will have to decide whether (1) to remove the person from the team or (2) to give the person one last chance. That is the subject of the next chapter.

The worksheets that conclude this chapter will help you through the five stages of our process for dealing with performance problems.

HOT WORKSHEET 9A

Diagnosing Performance Problems

Directions: Describe the performance problem; then determine whether it is a problem of ability, skill, or will (or a combination of these).

NAME OF DIRECT REPORT:

DATE:

DESCRIPTION OF PROBLEM:

Is This a Problem of Ability, Skill, or Will?

1. **Ability:** If the problem is ability, then your direct report's natural strengths are simply not a good match with some or all of the tasks and responsibilities in his or her current role.

   - **Does this apply to the present problem? If so, how?**

   - **Action:** In this case, your best option is to change the tasks and responsibilities that are a poor match. If you cannot do that, then you may have to remove the person from your team.

➥

HOT WORKSHEET 9A — CONCLUDED

2. **Skill:** If the problem is skill, then the person does not have sufficient training for some or all of the tasks and responsibilities in his or her current role.

   - **Does this apply to the present problem? If so, how?**

   - **Action:** Find the skill gaps and ensure the direct report immediately gets the training needed to do the job. If you cannot, you may have to remove the person from the team.

3. **Will:** Here, the person has an internal or external issue. If the problem seems internal (depression, for example), then your best option may be to recommend therapy or some form of employee services. However, often problems of will are problems of external motivation. In such a case, you must explore incentives that will re-engage the person.

   - **Does this apply to the present problem? If so, how?**

   - **Action:** If you cannot offer the necessary incentives or if, no matter what you offer, the problem continues, then you may have to remove the person from your team.

If you can analyze performance problems in these terms—ability, skill, and will—you should be able to move people quickly toward a solution.

HOT WORKSHEET 9B

Prepare for the Intervention Meeting

Directions: Before the meeting, follow the steps below and answer the questions provided.

1. Review your manager's notebook. Think about your prior meetings with this direct report. What patterns of poor performance have you already documented? What measures, if any, have you already taken to correct the problem?

2. Clarify exactly what's wrong. What is the first issue you are going to focus on?

3. Identify specific examples of the problem area you've identified. Do you have pertinent details such as times, places, and projects where the direct report failed to meet goals, make deadlines, and/or follow guidelines?

➡

HOT WORKSHEET 9B — CONCLUDED

4. Reconsider how you would categorize the problem. It is one of ability, skill, or will?

5. What concrete action steps are you willing to take?

6. What concrete action steps are you going to ask the direct report to take?

7. Before you proceed, consult an ally in HR to ensure you are following proper procedures. Who will you talk to? Make note of the guidance that you receive from HR:

HOT WORKSHEET 9C
Scripting the Intervention Conversation

Directions: After each guideline below, write down what you might say to the direct report in question.

Remember: By creating and rehearsing a script, you will find it easier to stay on track during your meeting and effectively address the direct report's arguments, excuses, and emotions. As you prepare your script, be sure to think of the excuses this person typically offers you for failing to meet deadlines or accomplish goals.

1. Make it clear that you are meeting to discuss a problem.

2. Remind the direct report that high performance is non-negotiable.

3. Identify the performance problem. Be as specific as you can, presenting the facts as you've documented them.

➡

4. Talk about the problem in terms of ability, skill, and will. Ask the direct report what he or she thinks. Share your own analysis.

5. Agree on a plan to improve the performance problem. Make sure you get the person's input, but be prepared to offer concrete suggestions.

6. Explain that you will be working much more closely with the person to help turn the problem around and create an upward spiral of performance and rewards.

HOT WORKSHEET 9D
Sample Performance Improvement Plan

Directions: Use this sample as a guide for recording a plan upon which the direct report and you have agreed. Be sure the direct report thoroughly understands the plan's contents before he or she signs it.

NAME OF DIRECT REPORT:

DATE:

Performance Issue Discussed:

Performance Improvement Agreed Upon:

GOALS	DEADLINES	GUIDELINES	COMMENTS

SIGNATURE (Direct Report):

SIGNATURE (Manager):

One Last Chance?
Removing the Stubborn Low Performer

WHAT IF, DESPITE your best efforts, you simply cannot turn around the performance problem of a direct report? What do you do? I believe, as strongly as I believe anything, that if you cannot help an employee improve, then you must get tough and, without delay, remove that person from your team. Is there any hope of one last chance at performance improvement? Yes, and our practical approach in this chapter is based on that hope. Still, the first option holds. You therefore must use your best business judgment to decide which course of action you will pursue:

- Immediate removal of the problem performer
- Final intervention—one last chance

Immediate Removal of the Problem Performer

Sometimes it is clear from your regular coaching sessions that the situation is hopeless. Perhaps the person's attitude has been consistently poor or even the slightest improvement has been impossible to achieve. When you hit situations like this, there are four reasons to remove the stubborn low performers ASAP:

1. They get paid. That's right. And they're soaking up valuable rewards that should be going to those who are performing at an acceptable level.

2. They cause problems that better performers have to fix. Don't fool yourself into believing that low performers are a net gain when it comes to productivity. And don't think that your best performers will weep to see the worst performers go. You're more likely to hear: "What took you so long? I've been cleaning up after that person far too long. Good riddance!"

3. They discourage high performers, who hate to work with them. The best performers want to work in a high-energy environment where everyone on the team is valuable and is pulling their own weight. When they see that low performance is accepted, they become demoralized, lose respect for management, and start looking to move to a high-performance team.

4. They send a terrible message to the rest of the team, your vendors, and your customers: "Low performance is an option here." Don't let them send that message. Instead, send another message: "High performance is the *only* option here."

Final Intervention—One Last Chance

Why would you give a stubborn low performer one last chance? Conversely, why wouldn't you? Here are the pros and cons of this option:

The Pros

- If you can turn the performer around, you'll save the organization and your team the costs of turn-over. These include . . .
  - the actual removal
  - any exit benefits
  - the loss of the recruiting and training investment
  - any downtime that results in the loss of a staff person
  - the recruiting and training costs of hiring a replacement

- You've already invested time, energy, and money in this person; if you invest a little bit more, then you might get a return on that investment.

- In the event of a dispute, your case might be stronger if you give the person one last chance before termination.

- The situation, the performer, and your own feelings may warrant going the extra mile and being extra fair.

- Your company may require you to give the performer one last chance.

The Cons

- If the performer is hopeless, the costs of turnover are actually a fiction. The primary costs of the bad hire have already been incurred. Retention will thus be more costly than termination.

- If the person is hopeless, you shouldn't throw good time, energy, and money after bad.

- If you've kept good contemporaneous records of your management interactions with this person and his or her failure to perform, then you probably don't need to give the person a last chance in order to strengthen your case. Your case is already strong.

- Depending on the situation and the performer, a last chance at improvement may turn into an opportunity for that person to bad-mouth you, the team, and the organization; to do bad work and cause problems; and to steal or commit acts of sabotage.

- Your company may forbid you to give the performer one last chance.

Based on these pros and cons and the particulars of each situation, you have to decide: Do you want to give the direct report a last chance, or not?

The Four-Step Approach to Final Intervention

If you decide to give the problem performer one last chance, you will need to conduct a "deal-breaker" meeting with the person. Here are the four steps involved:

1. Prepare for the deal-breaker meeting.
2. Script, rehearse, and conduct the meeting.
3. If agreement is reached, follow up aggressively.
4. If all else fails, terminate.

1. Prepare for the Deal-Breaker Meeting

You should be ready psychologically as well as tactically for the most difficult conversation you will ever hold with a direct report. Why? Because you may have to deal with all or some of the following:

- A barrage of excuses
- Accusations that you have unreasonable expectations
- Extreme emotions, from anger to tears to outright belligerence

With this in mind, be sure to follow these six guidelines:

- **First,** review your manager's notebook, especially the notes you've made since earnestly beginning your performance improvement efforts with this person.

- **Second,** review the direct report's performance improvement plan. Consider these questions:
  - In what areas did this person fail to improve?
  - Have you been coaching in all those areas?
  - Did you misdiagnose the problem?
  - Is the employee's ability to succeed still in the locus of his or her own control?
  - Have you exhausted all your options to help this person improve?

- **Third,** zero in on specific examples of how this person's performance problem has continued. If there have been slight improvements or small victories, point to those. But emphasize the details of exactly how the problem is continuing.

- **Fourth,** decide what concrete steps you will require for this direct report to continue as a team member. Make sure the steps are measurable. Use them to prepare a clear but simple "performance improvement contract." This contract represents the employee's last chance. By signing it, he or she is committing to improve performance and acknowledging that failure on that account means removal from the team.

  In the contract, you must spell out the commitments and deadlines that you expect from the person. Treat this as a legal document to be signed by the direct report, you, and another witness. A sample form for this purpose is provided at the end of this chapter.

- **Fifth,** consult again with your ally in HR. Ensure you are following proper procedures. For example, your company may have a customized form that you should use for the performance improvement contract instead of our sample form.

- **Sixth,** rally your allies. Ask a manager you know and trust to attend the meeting. This person will witness not only the meeting but also the signing of the performance improvement contract. Having another manager present as well as a contract in hand sends a strong message that you are serious about the meeting's "improve or remove" theme.

  You should probably plan to meet with the other manager beforehand to make sure you are dotting your "i's" and crossing your "t's." It would be also be a great idea to role-play your script with your ally-manager to practice and to get feedback.

2. Script, Rehearse, and Conduct the Meeting

By creating a script for your deal-breaker conversation and then rehearsing it, you will be more apt to stay on track during the meeting. In your conversation, you'll need to do the following:

- **First,** make it clear that you are meeting to discuss the direct report's lack of progress on the problem and that the situation cannot continue this way.

- **Second,** explain that the situation is serious enough that you've consulted HR, gotten approval to proceed with the conversation, and put HR on notice that termination may result if the problem is not resolved. Also explain that you've brought the other manager with you because you want to make sure there is an independent third party to witness the conversation.

- **Third,** offer specific examples of the performance failures that have occurred since you started working on the problem with the person. Explain the negative impact that the problem is causing and some of the specific outcomes.

- **Fourth,** let the individual know that you have exhausted your options. Recap all the things you've tried to do to facilitate improved performance, and explain that now you are left with only one option: If the individual doesn't make a 100 percent commitment to improve immediately, you'll have to remove him or her from the team immediately.

- **Fifth,** explain that you've decided to give the direct report one last chance. This is his or her last opportunity to turn the problem around.

- **Sixth,** explain the concrete actions—goals and deadlines—to which the individual must agree in order to remain on the team.

- **Seventh,** present the performance improvement contract. Make it clear that the condition for continued employment is a 100 percent commitment to improvement and 100 percent fulfillment of the goals and deadlines in the contract. Go over the contract and explain that if the person commits to improving performance and signs the contract, you will continue your intense coaching and hold him or her strictly accountable. One failure will result in termination until the person has built a substantial track record of dramatic improvement.

  There's no getting away from it: You will have to make a dramatic investment of your time to turn this employee around; so make sure it is understood that without 100 percent commitment and success, the person will be terminated immediately.

- **Eighth,** hold your ground if the employee refuses to sign the agreement. Use the broken-record technique. Keep repeating the lines: "As a condition of your continued employment, you have to make a 100 percent commitment to improving performance. Signing this document is proof of your commitment."

  Let the person make excuses and throw obstacles at you until he or she is blue in the face. Just keep coming back with those lines. Eventually, the person will get the message and sign the document— or quit. If the employee does not sign and does not quit, you have no options left: You must terminate that person.

- **Ninth,** if the employee signs the contract, you and your witness should co-sign it. Make sure that all three of you walk away from the meeting with a copy. You should also give your ally in HR a copy as well as an update on the situation.

3. If Agreement Is Reached, Follow Up Aggressively

If the direct report signs the document, you will have to follow up aggressively.

- **First,** intensify your hands-on approach by shrinking the circle of empowerment and meeting frequently with the direct report for coaching sessions. Give the person a chance to succeed, but do not tolerate the slightest failure. If the person fails, remove him or her immediately.

- **Second,** if the direct report begins to improve, keep the pressure on. Set relatively small goals with short deadlines, and spell out every guideline and parameter for every goal.

  As the person demonstrates improved performance, consistently meeting the goals and deadlines as specified, consider meeting with him or her to discuss the improvement. Also think about reducing your hands-on intensity and slowly enlarging the circle of empowerment. At this point, you will have a tremendous management success story to tell!

4. If All Else Fails, Terminate

To be sure, firing someone is one of the most unpleasant, scary things you'll ever have to do as a manager. But if you've gone through all the steps that we have covered so far in this book and the person is still not improving, you have no choice but to terminate. You owe it to yourself, your team, and your organization.

As for the process of termination, your organization probably has steps for you to follow. Learn them, and make sure to follow the designated process closely.

The Big Excuses: "Red Tape" and "Fear of Litigation"

If you're reluctant to terminate because of "red tape" and "fear of litigation," you're hiding behind excuses and need to realize that.

You can deal with red tape by simply figuring out what the rules are and going to the trouble to follow them.

With regard to litigation, this is usually a red herring. Disgruntled employees with a litigious bent can always sue the company, whether they have a legitimate discrimination claim or not. That doesn't mean they're going to succeed. And it doesn't matter how well you manage or how much you try to do for your people, there will always be disgruntled employees. But if you manage people well, hold them to a high standard, help them work toward success, and reward them when they do succeed, you'll have far fewer disgruntled employees. More of your people will be satisfied high-level performers who exert pressure on others to become the same. Low-level performers will be minimized because you'll be dealing promptly with performance problems. And if you get rid of the hopelessly low performers, you'll have even fewer disgruntled employees.

Staying on Safe Legal Ground

The key to staying on safe legal ground is simple:

- Know what you cannot do.
- Know what you can do.
- Know how to do things right.

There are many impermissible reasons for distinguishing between and among employees. Performance is not one of them. As long as you can demonstrate that all employee rewards and detriments are based solely on work performance, there is no basis for a claim of unlawful discrimination.

The important thing is to use clear performance standards. Stick to measurable goals, concrete guidelines, and specific deadlines. Apply the same standards to every employee. And keep good written records that are brief, straightforward, and simple. If you dot your "i's" and cross your "t's," keep good notes of your interactions with employees, and ensure you don't discriminate unlawfully, you'll have nothing to worry about.

How do you find out what you can and cannot do? You don't have to be a labor lawyer or a human resources expert to navigate through the rules and regulations, but you do have to know where to go to get the support you need to make this work. You need to find allies in your organization's HR and Legal departments—and don't forget your own boss. Some counterintuitive sources for allies include union representatives and onsite EEO officers. Don't think of these people as adversaries; instead, try to work with them.

In seeking information, always ask, "How can I do this?" rather than, "Can I do this?" Asking for permission always results in a yes or no answer, which leaves your hands tied. In asking how you can do something, you're asking for very different information: a solution, a way of untying your hands.

The following guidelines will help you deal with the issue of legality.

Guidelines for Staying Safe Legally

1. Don't discriminate unlawfully. It is unlawful in the United States (or in certain states) to discriminate in hiring, managing, rewarding, or firing employees on the basis of:

   - Race
   - Color
   - Religion
   - Age
   - Sexual orientation
   - Marital status

- Gender
- National origin
- Disability
- Veteran status
- Political beliefs

2. Learn what you can do. It is entirely legal, permissible, and fair to discriminate in hiring, managing, rewarding, or firing employees on the basis of work performance.

3. Know how to do it. Base rewards and detriments solely on work performance. Apply the same standards to every employee. Keep good written records that are brief, straightforward, and simple. Include in all your notes the employee's name, the date, and what you've discussed. And stick to measurable goals, parameters, and deadlines.

4. Create a "go to" list of allies. Learn to ask, "How can I do this?" rather than, "Can I do this?" For sources of go-to allies, consider the following:

- Departments such as Human Resources and Legal
- Your boss
- EEO officer
- Union officials

HOT WORKSHEET 10A

Preparing for the Last-Chance Meeting

Directions: Before the meeting, follow the steps below. Use the write-in spaces to record your notes on each step and to answer the questions provided.

1. Review your manager's notebook, especially the notes you've made since initiating performance improvement efforts with the direct report. Are your notes in order?

2. Does the direct report have a performance improvement plan from your prior efforts to improve performance? If so, review it. In what areas has this person failed to improve?

3. Zero in on specific examples of how the performance problem has continued. If you would find it helpful, note those examples below.

4. Decide what concrete steps the direct report must take to continue as a team member. Make sure the steps are measurable. Use them to prepare a clear but simple "performance improvement contract." (See the sample contract at the end of this chapter.)

➡

5. Consult with your ally in HR. Is there a procedure you should follow? Does the organization require certain paperwork? Whose approval will you need for termination? Does the organization have a formal document, such as a customized performance improvement contract or a written warning, that you should use?

6. Arrange for a trustworthy manager to be present at the meeting as a witness and to co-sign the performance improvement contract. Whom might you ask to fill this role?

7. Hold a meeting with your ally-manager and your ally in HR to make sure everything is in order.

8. Role-play your meeting script with your ally-manager to practice and to get feedback. Do you need to make any improvements to the script?

HOT WORKSHEET 10B

Scripting the Last-Chance Meeting

Directions: After each guideline below, write down what you might say to the direct report in question.

1. Make it clear that you are meeting because the performance problem you have been working on with the direct report is not improving, and that the situation cannot continue.

2. Explain that the situation is serious enough that you've consulted HR, gotten approval to proceed with the present conversation, and put HR on notice that termination may result if the problem is not resolved. Also explain that you've brought the other manager with you to act as an independent third-party witness to the conversation.

3. Offer specific examples of the performance failures that have occurred since you started working on this problem with the person. Explain the negative impact the problem is having on the workplace, and specify some of the outcomes.

4. Recap all that you've tried to do to help the person improve performance. Then explain that you must get a 100 percent commitment from the person to improve immediately or you will have to remove him or her from the team immediately.

➡

HOT WORKSHEET 10B — CONCLUDED

5. Offer the direct report one last chance.

6. Explain the concrete actions—goals and deadlines—to which the individual must agree in order to remain on the team.

7. Present the performance improvement contract. Make it clear that the condition for continued employment is a 100 percent commitment to improvement and 100 percent fulfillment of the goals and deadlines in the contract.

8. If the employee refuses to sign the agreement, keep repeating: "As a condition of your continued employment, you have to make a 100 percent commitment to improving performance. Signing this document is proof of your commitment." (You may want to write this statement out and memorize it.)

Remember: If the employee signs the contract, you and your witness should co-sign it. Make sure that all three of you walk away from the meeting with a copy. You should also give your ally in HR a copy as well as an update on the situation.

HOT WORKSHEET 10C
Sample Performance Improvement Contract

Directions: Use this sample as a guide for the direct report's contract.

PERFORMANCE IMPROVEMENT CONTRACT

This is a contract between _____ (manager) and
_____ (employee) as witnessed by _____.

It is understood and agreed that the employee will make a 100 percent commitment to achieve the following:

GOALS	DEADLINES	GUIDELINES	COMMENTS

It is understood and agreed that the employee's achievement of the goals, deadlines, and guidelines listed above is an absolute requirement for continued employment at _____ (company). It is also understood and agreed that the employee's failure to achieve any of the goals, deadlines, and guidelines listed above will result in his or her immediate termination of employment.

SIGNATURE (Employee):
NAME: **DATE:**

SIGNATURE (Manager):
NAME: **DATE:**

SIGNATURE (Witness):
NAME: **DATE:**

One Last HOT Review

WHY IS IT BECOMING more and more difficult to manage people? Because everybody is under more pressure and people are trying to get their needs met. Managers are expected to achieve greater results with fewer resources. Welcome to the *real* new economy. As we have seen in this pocket guide, and as we will quickly review here, HOT Management offers you a way to deal with that reality effectively.

The HOT Approach and Guidelines

HOT Management is based on 10 years of research on the front lines of the changing workplace. In that workplace today, managers are losing their old-fashioned, long-term hierarchical power, but they have many opportunities to draw on new sources of short-term transactional power. When managers take a hands-on and transactional (HOT) approach to managing, they can do much more for employees. At the same time, they can require much more from employees. This results in much higher productivity, quality, and morale, and better retention of high-level performers.

HOT Management draws on the style, techniques, skills, best practices, and habits of the most effective managers in today's extremely demanding workplace. It offers 12 guidelines for making the HOT transition:

1. Become highly knowledgeable about the tasks and responsibilities of your direct reports.

2. Start spending time with every direct report in daily coaching sessions.

3. Use your coaching time to talk about the work people are doing. Be sure to focus on performance standards and concrete assignments—that means talking about clear goals and deadlines.

4. Provide direction, guidance, support, and coaching on a regular basis.

5. Start a written tracking system so that you can monitor and measure every individual's performance on a daily basis. This will help you reward success and address failure.

6. Understand, accept, and embrace the new reality that managing people has become a day-to-day negotiation.

7. Embrace the fact that everything that is not a deal-breaker is open to negotiation. Decide what

your deal-breakers are—what's not open to negotiation—and then be prepared to negotiate regularly about everything else.

8. Whenever possible, tie financial rewards and detriments to measurable instances of employee performance—and to nothing else.

9. Be creative and use your discretion and discretionary resources to tie nonfinancial rewards, incentives, and benefits to measurable instances of employee performance.

10. Look for every employee's "needle in a haystack" and use those needles to make custom deals with individual performers in exchange for exceptional performance.

11. Have the discipline and guts to enforce every deal you make, and don't flinch when it comes to providing the promised rewards and detriments.

12. And remember: You cannot be hands-on without being transactional, and you cannot be transactional without being hands-on.

Introducing Your Team to HOT Management

Before you undertake a major shift in your management style and start implementing HOT Management, prepare your team for the changes ahead. How are you going to do that?

1. Hold a team meeting to announce the change.
2. Hold an initial one-on-one meeting with each team member.

This approach will help you to make the transition.

The Daily Coaching Session

Ideally, you would meet with every single direct report every single day. If that is impossible, you may meet less often, but you *must* meet with every direct report at least once a week.

Regular coaching sessions are essential for at least five reasons:

1. Preparing for them forces you and your direct report to remain up-to-speed and up-to-date about the key details of the direct report's tasks and responsibilities. When managers stay in the loop, everybody stays clear and thoughtful.

2. Regular coaching sessions will allow you to monitor changes in each direct report's workload, pace, level of difficulty, and corresponding needs.

3. They will let you know when you need to step up guidance and support, and when you can back off. You'll thus be able to apply the right amount of pressure to keep each person focused on ambitious goals and deadlines.

4. Regular coaching sessions will put you in a great position to troubleshoot, to bring in additional resources, or to change direction when necessary.

5. They will help you measure success and failure and steer rewards to the right people at the right times.

But that is not all. Perhaps the most essential thing about regular coaching sessions is the very act of making time several times a week to discuss expectations. This is a tremendous source of psychological accountability and the key to practical accountability.

Conducting regular coaching sessions is the most important discipline of HOT Management. You have to make the time for these sessions. And you have to make holding the sessions a habit.

The Manager's Notebook

The second most important discipline of HOT Management is documentation. This means keeping a running log of your coaching sessions (and any special sessions) with every direct report. The best approach is to organize and keep a "manager's notebook."

Organize the notebook as a tracking system, both chronologically and by person. Then keep track of the essential details of your discussions about the following:

1. Reminders about overall performance standards
2. Goals
3. Deadlines
4. Guidelines and parameters
5. Anticipating and planning for resource needs
6. Anticipating and planning to avoid problems
7. Questions asked by your direct report
8. Requests made by your direct report
9. Any quid pro quo you have promised in exchange for specific performance
10. Any other special issues that come up

Whether you use an old-fashioned paper notebook or an electronic format for your notes, remember that the idea is to find an approach that works easily for you so you can turn it into a habit. The key is to be disciplined about keeping detailed contemporaneous records of your regular coaching sessions.

Do More for People and They Will Do More for You

To be effective as a HOT manager, you must be able to do more for your direct reports. However, you must also have the discipline to do more for your direct reports *only* when they do more for you. This is the art of the quid pro quo: "Here's what I need from you.

What do you need from me?" With HOT Management, that art requires two basic kinds of bargaining chips:

1. Money to use for short-term cash bonuses
2. Resources to use as short-term nonfinancial bonuses

If you want to take the bargaining-chip approach one step further, then you're ready to make custom deals with your high-level performers. This involves finding and using "needles in a haystack"—the wants and needs of the individual performers. Once found, the "needles" are useful when a direct report presents you with a special request or when you have a special request for a direct report. You can review the person's "needles" and determine whether you can offer a win-win transaction: "I'll do this for you, if you do [x, y, z] for me." Use such deals to drive high performers to reach ever more ambitious levels of achievement.

Of course, custom deals often require that you make special arrangements. But in most organizations, no matter what the rules are, special arrangements of all sorts happen all the time. How do they happen? Someone makes them happen. That someone could be you.

Dealing With Performance Problems

What do you do when, despite your regular coaching, a direct report fails to meet the performance standards and the daily goals and deadlines that the both of you have agreed on? The number one rule is, you cannot let people off the hook. Leniency with performance problems will diminish your credibility and undermine the team. If you don't deal with performance problems immediately and aggressively, then you will do a disservice to yourself, your team, and every person on the team. The person you will let down the most, of course, is the direct report whose performance is failing.

Remember our five-step process for dealing with performance problems:

1. Intensify your hands-on approach, narrowing the circle of empowerment.

2. If the first step fails, then diagnose the problem.

3. Prepare to engage the direct report in a performance improvement intervention.

4. Script, rehearse, and conduct the intervention.

5. Be aggressive about follow-up and try to reverse the downward spiral of performance.

One Last Chance?

What if you simply cannot turn around the performance problem of a direct report? What do you do? In such a situation, you are left with only two options:

- Immediate removal of the problem performer
- Final intervention—one last chance

You must use your best business judgment to decide which one of these two options you will pursue.

Remember: If you opt to give the problem performer one last chance, you will need to conduct a "deal-breaker" meeting with the person, following these four steps:

1. Prepare for the deal-breaker meeting.
2. Script, rehearse, and conduct the meeting.
3. If agreement is reached, follow up aggressively.
4. If all else fails, terminate the person.

Don't be reluctant to terminate because of "red tape" and "fear of litigation"—these are simply excuses to hide behind. Deal with red tape by figuring out what the rules are and going to the trouble to follow them. As for litigation, make sure you know what you cannot do, what you can do, and how to do what you can do properly.

In Conclusion . . .

If you practice the techniques of HOT Management, they will become skills. If you practice those skills consistently, they will become habits. And mark my words: You will see dramatic improvements in productivity, quality, morale, and retention of high-level performers. If you want more information about HOT Management, just contact us through our website at www.rainmakerthinking.com. Until then, I wish you good skills and good habits!